Dorset FAMILIES

Rodney Legg

DORSET
BOOKS

First published in Great Britain in 2002

Dedicated to Tony Poyntz-Wright, of an ancient family,
who has walked the countryside with me.

British Library Cataloguing-in-Publication Data
A CIP record for this title is available from the British Library

ISBN 1 871164 46 X

DORSET BOOKS
Official publisher to Dorset County Council

Halsgrove House
Lower Moor Way
Tiverton, Devon EX16 6SS
Tel: 01884 243242
Fax: 01884 243325
email: sales@halsgrove.com
website: www.halsgrove.com

Printed and bound in Great Britain by Bookcraft Ltd, Midsomer Norton

INTRODUCTION

Families here are those linked to the principal county seats. Since my first writings began to appear in print, four decades ago, I have gathered stories of Dorset characters of all occupations and periods. They are far too many and varied to bring between two covers other than with potted listings looking like a fusion of the telephone book and the electoral roll.

There had to be a pragmatic answer. In order to achieve a degree of dispassionate selection I decided to include those whose existence revolved around what our Victorian ancestors would have called the county seats. These main mansions, mostly ancestral rather than stately homes, conveniently link people and place.

In the process my own Dorset links failed the property test. I mention them now as an example of how ordinary lives mix with those of the rich and powerful. John Hardy, my great-grandmother's brother from Wareham, was transported to Australia for theft at the Lent Assize in Dorchester which convicted the Tolpuddle Martyrs. Giving crucial evidence in 1834, of unlawful oath-taking against the six union members, was distant relative Edward Legg. In these pages, however, it is only the prime persecutor, landowner James Frampton of Moreton House, whose story is told.

Likewise the Thomas Hardy who appears in his own right is of the Hardy Monument, Nelson's flag captain at the Battle of Trafalgar, rather than an internationally known author. For all his genteel aspirations, Thomas Hardy the writer was born in a thatched cottage, and Thomas Masterman Hardy the sailor came into the world in Kingston Russell House (though his father only rented it). There is an irony there that writer Thomas would have appreciated as he created the great English novels about the national obsession with class.

What unfolds, surprising me at times when I traced some of the more obscure leads, is the interwoven nature of the lives of the families that not only owned most of Dorset but also wielded power nationally and established dynasties. Britain's top families are writ large in Dorset.

The Cecils at Cranborne have the Ashley Coopers next door at Wimborne St Giles where the names also remain the same after half a millennium. For the Churchills, John progressed from Round Chimneys Farm in the Blackmore Vale to Blenheim Palace, and descendant Winston returned to Canford – almost losing his life – and married off his son to Pamela Digby at Minterne. The Russells rose from obscurity by a totally chance royal meeting at Wolferton House which resulted in John Russell being given the Bedford earldom and moving on to Woburn Abbey from which the family has never needed to look back. The powerful Pitts evolved into the Pitt-Rivers line when the archaeological General inherited a landed fortune against all the odds. These are their stories.

LOCATION MAP

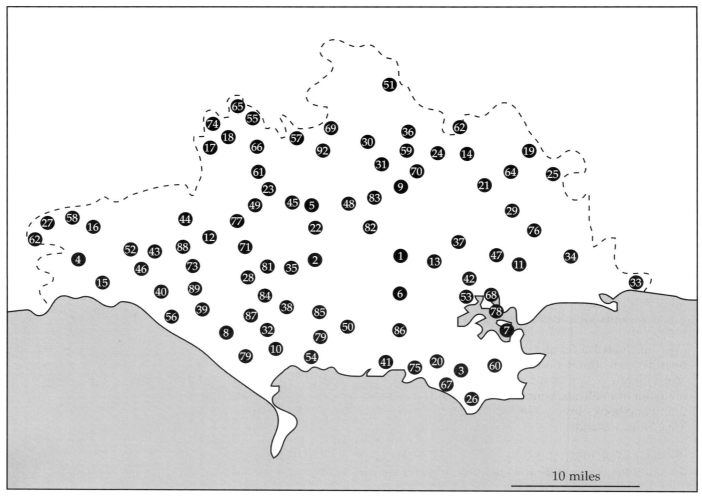

10 miles

1 Anderson	24 Eastbury	47 Merley	70 Stepleton
2 Athelhampton	25 Edmondsham	48 Milton	71 Sydling
3 Barnston	26 Encombe	49 Minterne	72 Thornhill
4 Bettiscombe	27 Forde	50 Moreton	73 Toller Fratrum
5 Bingham's Melcombe	28 Frampton	51 Motcombe House	74 Trent
6 Bloxworth	29 Gaunt's	52 Parnham	75 Tyneham
7 Branksea	30 Hammoon	53 Post Green	76 Uddens
8 Bridehead	31 Hanford	54 Poxwell	77 Upcerne
9 Bryanston	32 Herringston	55 Poyntington	78 Upton
10 Came	33 Highcliffe	56 Puncknowle	79 Waddon
11 Canford	34 Hurn	57 Purse Caundle	80 Warmwell
12 Chantmarle	35 Ilsington	58 Racedown	81 Waterston
13 Charborough	36 Iwerne Minster	59 Ranston	82 Whatcombe
14 Chettle	37 Kingston Lacy	60 Rempstone	83 Winterborne Clenston
15 Chideock	38 Kingston Maurward	61 Round Chimneys	84 Wolfeton
16 Childhay	39 Kingston Russell	62 Rushmore	85 Woodsford Castle
17 Clifton Maybank	40 Loders	63 Sadborow	86 Woolbridge
18 Compton	41 Lulworth	64 Saint Giles	87 Wrackleford
19 Cranborne	42 Lytchett Matravers	65 Sandford Orcas	88 Wraxall
20 Creech	43 Mapperton	66 Sherborne	89 Wynford
21 Crichel	44 Melbury	67 Smedmore	
22 Dewlish	45 Melcombe Horsey	68 South Lytchett	
23 Duntish	46 Melplash	69 Stalbridge	

ANDERSON MANOR

Turberville — Morton — Tregonwell — Gratrix — Tabor — Cholmondeley — Bullivant — Isaac

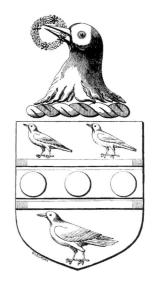

Built by John Tregonwell of Milton Abbey in 1622, this small Jacobean house in the Winterborne valley north-east of Bere Regis is on the site of one of the Turberville family homes. It had passed to Sir George Morton of Milborne St Andrew by the time that Tregonwell acquired the estate in 1620. The new home, in neat brick, comprises three E-shaped wings of perfect symmetry.

John Tregonwell's retirement went through an unsettling time in the Civil War when younger son Thomas Tregonwell's royalist affiliations brought about the threat of sequestration, in 1645, which was only lifted after the payment of £3735.

The Tregonwell family retained ownership until 1910 when Mrs Gordon Gratrix bought the house and set about stripping out various accretions as she restored it to something approaching its original state. The next owner was Colonel John Clement Tabor, followed by Hugh Cholmondeley, during whose time it was requisitioned for the Second World War on behalf of Acting Admiral Louis Mountbatten and Combined Operations.

The Tregonwell arms were brought to Anderson by John Tregonwell, from Milton Abbas in 1625

They instigated a Small Scale Raiding Force for cross-Channel raids, which became No.62 Commando and counted Captain Gustavus March-Phillips and Major Geoffrey Appleyard among its first heroes. Their notable success, operating out of Poole Harbour, was to seize seven German wireless operators and their code-books from a U-boat signal station in the Casquets Lighthouse, in the Channel Islands.

Post-war, after 1952, Anderson Manor was the home of Eric Bullivant, and of John and Rosemary Isaac towards the end of the century.

ATHELHAMPTON HALL

Martyn — Brune — Long — Long-Wellesley — Wood — de Lafontaine — Cochrane — Harmsworth — Phillips — Cooke

One of the great country houses of Dorset, the early Tudor Athelhampton Hall was built by Sir William Martyn, in about 1485. He received a licence to build a fortified manor house, with battlements and towers, in 160 acres of former deer park between Puddletown and Tolpuddle. Sir William lies in the Athelhampton Aisle of St Mary's parish church in Puddletown and his son, Christopher Martyn, extended the house into the West Wing with its Great Chamber (the drawing room) and Long Gallery. There are many versions of the chained-ape crest of the Martyn family, and its motto, which became synonymous with the house and have been adopted by later owners: 'He who looks at Martyn's ape, Martyn's ape shall look at him.'

The Martyn male line ended with the death of Nicholas Martyn, in 1595, when the property was shared between his four daughters. The controlling interest became absorbed into the Brune family, ancestors of the Prideaux-Brunes of Cornwall and Dorset. Henry Brune also produced daughters and one married

Sir Ralph Bankes of Kingston Lacy in 1661. Sir Ralph sold Athelhampton to Sir Robert Long, in 1665, and from Sir James Long it passed to William Long-Wellesley, fourth Earl of Mornington (1788–1857), whose son sold it to George Wood. He had the superlative timbering of the Great Hall repaired and restored.

Alfred Cart de Lafontaine did something similar for the surroundings, embellishing the grounds with late Victorian walled gardens. He was followed by George Cochrane in 1918 and the Honourable Mrs Esmond Harmsworth in 1930. In 1947 she married divorcee Sir John Blunt and they moved to Waldron, near Heathfield, Sussex.

The publisher of *Polemic*, Rodney Phillips, bought Athelhampton in 1949, bringing about its brief Cubist period, with the paintings of his mother-in-law, Marevna Vorobrev. It was Bristol surgeon Robert Victor Cooke, who bought the house in 1957, and established the new Parliamentary dynasty. He gave the house to son Robert and daughter-in-law Jenifer on their wedding day in 1966. Sir Robert Cooke MP (1930–87), who was always known as Robin, introduced

the Historic Buildings Bill in the House of Commons in 1963. He took an active role in setting up English Heritage and at home, with Lady Cooke (the daughter of Evelyn King MP), recreated the decor and found furniture of the sort that would have graced the house if it had not been through such a multiplicity of owners. Among the treasures are Queen Charlotte's harpsichord (in the Great Chamber), dating from 1761, and the bed of the great statesman the Marquis of Curzon (1859–1925), in the State Bedroom which dates from the sixteenth century and came from Montacute House, and a collection of Worcester porcelain.

Table-tomb in Puddletown Church to an anonymous member of the Martyn family from Athelhampton

Athelhampton has proved to be a phoenix. It was partially thanks to the present author that the scale of destruction – and therefore the degree of subsequent restoration – were somewhat exaggerated when it became national news that Athelhampton Hall was being consumed by fire on the morning of 2 November 1992. The media began telephoning the moment the fire engines started to arrive and I listed the contents from undated guidebooks to the house.

'So it was you!' said present owner Patrick Cooke in a mild-mannered rebuke. 'I wondered where the information came from. Some of the items survived but others on the list were items that had been sold years before.'

Damage to the grand house was also over-stated. It was left partially gutted rather than utterly ruined and the damaged parts are now so skilfully rebuilt that they merge with the original fabric without visual clues. What matters is that the grace and grandeur survives intact. The finest Tudor stonework, framing a house of the first order, is further enriched by the presence of its owner-in-residence who makes a practice of being available to his visiting public on a regular basis. Patrick Cooke has the presence and confidence that come from Harrow and these roots.

Dorchester Hospital was his 'surrogate birthplace' on 1 June 1967. He worked for Christie's, the art auctioneers, and accountants Redman and Roker at Poole. Then he was due for a spell at Kew Gardens but fate and destiny intervened.

Patrick's father, Sir 'Robin' Cooke, was the epitome of a do-it-yourself landowner, being as hands-on as anyone you could imagine, as I saw for myself when I gave an impromptu talk at a seminar to cover the period blacked out by a power-cut. He also produced one of the great London books with a

Stately home owner Patrick Cooke in the Great Hall at Athelhampton

fulsome coffee-table celebration of the Palace of Westminster. Robin's early death, on 6 January 1987, was followed by his widow, Jenifer, marrying former Taunton MP, Sir Edward du Cann. 'On her departure, in a way, I started running the place,' Patrick told me. His sister Louise, born in 1970, had gone into medicine.

Jenny Cooke also died cruelly early, on 10 January 1995, and that suddenly left Patrick in charge of everything. 'I always had an idea that I would take the place over in the twenty-first century but it all happened ten years earlier,' he said. 'It's a big place to organise. There are days you only just cope with, and always the unexpected. No two days are ever the same here. The place evolves and was so different in only four years, ignoring the fire. There is an evolution going on all the time.'

Patrick Cooke handles questions with ease and answers with precision, giving facts and dates in a manner that would do credit to an historian, probably resulting from his accountancy background. He hopes that classics will come back into favour as a result of people's having to struggle with the language.

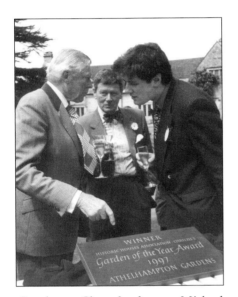

Cranborne Chase landowner Michael Pitt-Rivers (left) makes his point to Patrick Cooke at Athelhampton in 1997

The legacy of the fire of 1992 was the arrival of carpenter Richard Bolton, from Netherbury, who stayed in the North Wing as the in-house furniture restorer. There is also a Patrick Cooke addition with a London flavour. This is a room with Augustus Pugin wallpaper and fire-grate, with the latter having been discovered in a barn by auctioneer Guy Schwinge of Duke's of Dorchester, not that he realised it was by the eminent Victorian designer who resurrected the Palace of Westminster after its great fire. 'Though he didn't know exactly what it was, two or three others did, so it went for rather more than the estimate. but I was able to bring it here, to a good home, into a Parliamentary setting.'

Dorchester picture framer Olive Monahan has a knack for making paintings and prints blend with the decor: 'I tell her where it is to go in the house and it comes back with a frame that is in sympathy with its surroundings.' Outdoors there has been a return to the formal concepts of the first Elizabethans. A new rose garden has been established and the shrubbery reinvigorated beside Queen Victoria Walk. Patrick was moving on to clearing scrub beside the River Piddle: 'I'm hoping for great things for that as well, clearing brambles so that you can see across to a backdrop of trees and beyond, to deepen the view.'

Marketing is another expertise, as he produced the latest version of the Athelhampton guide, correcting much of the misinformation which I had unwittingly fed to national newspapers in response to their panic phone calls as the house was burning. The fire wasn't the first time the house had received media attention.

Sleuth was filmed here, in 1972, with Michael Caine and Laurence Olivier. There are also ghosts, of Martyn's ape – which appears in a stained-glass window as well as memorialised in stone – and of numerous owners and servants. 'I've written down all I've heard about them,' Patrick said, 'though I haven't seen any myself. My father used to say he had but I think he just liked the idea of them.'

His parents established the welcoming ethos: 'It was taken up in a very joint way. People appreciated seeing my parents here and I also try to be available for visitors, if only on one day a week. It makes all the difference in atmosphere and heightens the experience. The public has its expectations of how things should be, but not how these expectations come about. They want the most unusual things. These extend to 20 questions that are not in the guidebook.'

The biggest improvement to the setting came with the removal of the A35 trunk road to a dual-carriageway through the undulating chalklands north of the house. Patrick was already anticipating the improvement and looking forward to taking advantage of it by inviting the Bournemouth Symphony Orchestra to play on the lawn: 'The ambience of the place will improve enormously. Cars are not so bad but it is exceedingly noisy with heavy lorries. All that is to be moved to the other side of the flood-plain.'

'Don't mention the fire,' seems to be the best advice to prospective visitors, but Patrick Cooke is under no illusions that he will ever hear the last of it: 'They will go on asking about the fire for the next goodness knows how many years. I'm thinking of having a fines box.'

BARNSTON HOUSE

Estoke — Clavell — Bond

Dating back to 1280, this almost complete manor house from the reign of Edward II is one of three such ancient houses in the Isle of Purbeck, with the others being Godlingston and Scowles on the other side of Corfe Castle. Barnston, at Church Knowle, was built by the Estoke family who held it until the reign of Henry VI. It then passed through marriage to John Clavell of Leeson House at Langton Matravers. His wife, Joan Wyot, also owned Smedmore, but Barnston was the Clavell family home until the early-seventeenth century when they moved to the seaside at Smedmore. During their time at Barnston it was given its Tudor second storey, resting on massive and moulded oak beams, in the mid-sixteenth century.

Since 1852, Barnston has housed a branch of the Bond family, from Creech Grange.

Dairymaid and washing on the line in C. M. Colvile's back view of Barnston House

The ancient south side of Barnston House painted by C. M. Colvile in 1853

BETTISCOMBE MANOR

Pinney — Pretor — Conran

The macabre resident of Bettiscombe Manor is a skull that has to stay with the house

The 350-year association between Bettiscombe and the Pinneys dates back to half a century before 1694 when the present house was built by John Pinney who had succeeded Thomas Fuller as rector of nearby Broadwindsor. John Pinney died in 1705 and his son Nathaniel Pinney is credited with the addition of a Doric pediment and entablature as a classical hood to the south doorway. His son, Azariah Pinney, inherited the house in 1724 and may well have been responsible for the oak panelling and other woodwork which turned the house from a farm into a small country house.

Two of their relatives had thrown in their lot with the Duke of Monmouth's insurrection of 1685 which ended with defeat at the Battle of Sedgemoor. Both were condemned by Judge Jeffreys at his Bloody Assize but their death sentences were commuted to penal transportation. Azariah Pinney and John Pinney found themselves in the West Indies where one, at least, would prosper. Azariah's son, John Pinney who died in 1720, was Chief Justice of Nevis.

His son, John Frederick Pinney, returned to Bettiscombe to join his English cousin Azariah Pinney — the owner of the house from 1724 — and became Member of Parliament for Bridport. A family legend says that the Bettiscombe skull, displayed in a niche in the house, is that of his faithful Negro servant, though a modern pathologist concluded from its shape that it had come from one of Dorset's Bronze Age barrows. Azariah Pinney, a widower, died childless in 1760 and was followed in 1762 by John Frederick Pinney, who had never married.

The estate passed to a cousin, John Pretor, who had been High Sheriff of Dorset at the exceptionally early age of twenty-four. In order to inherit he was required to assume the Pinney surname. John Pretor Pinney threw his energies into promoting the family's diverse interests and directly managed their estates in the West Indies before he returned to Europe, in the late 1780s, and retired to Bristol. His home is now a museum, The Georgian House, at 7 Great George Street.

Set in the hilly hinterland directly inland from Lyme Regis and Charmouth, the English end of the Bettiscombe estate included the hill-fort of Pilsdon Pen, which at 908 feet above sea level is the highest point in Dorset. It was sold to the National Trust by Michael Pinney in 1979 and Bettiscombe Manor is now the home of Caroline Conran.

BINGHAM'S MELCOMBE

Turberville — Bingham — Bosworth Smith — Grogan — Hopwood — Southborough — Langham

Men of action and destiny have been produced in quantity from the premier country house in the gentle heart of the Dorset Downs. In the parish of Melcombe Horsey, where the once strategic Dorsetshire Gap is now one of the loneliest spots in the county, Bingham's Melcombe takes its name from a family that held sway there for 680 years and remains in the media eye thanks to a certain Earl of Lucan and a botched attack intended for the Countess of Lucan.

Bingham's Melcombe, home of the Bingham family for 680 years, in 1857

Before them the Turbervilles held Melcombe until heiress Lucy, daughter of Sir Robert Turberville, married Robert Bingham and brought the name to Dorset early in the thirteenth century. Robert's father was Sir Ralph Bingham and they lived within sight of the county, with their Somerset home of Sutton Bingham lying in the valley between the Dorset parishes of Halstock and Ryme Intrinseca. An uncle had been Bishop of Salisbury from 1229 to 1246.

For the next seven centuries the prominent members of the family tended to be soldiers or diplomats. The most notable, in the sixteenth century, was Sir Richard Bingham who, even by the standards of his time, was regarded as a practising sadist who 'knew no mercy' in his suppression of Irish insurgents and the wholesale slaughter of Spanish refugees. He died in Dublin in 1599, as Marshal of Ireland, and has his cenotaph in Westminster Abbey.

Bingham's Melcombe is a Queen Mary and Elizabethan country house, with grounds worthy of a stately home, including the oldest and biggest yew hedge in Britain – a gigantic wave of blurred topiary – with much of the architecture resulting from rebuilding by Robert Bingham, the elder brother of Sir Richard. The Bingham who put the house in jeopardy, but chose the winning side, was

The arms of Bingham whose title is the Lucan earldom

Plates, weapons and portraits on the wall at Bingham's Melcombe in 1915

The Bingham arms above a window in the Tudor gable overlooking the inner courtyard at Bingham's Melcombe in 1924

The yew hedge at Bingham's Melcombe, the biggest in Britain, in 1935

Sir John Trenchard of Bloxworth was principal Secretary of State to King William III

John Bingham who loaned it for the headquarters of local elements of the Parliamentary Army in the Civil War and personally took charge of the second siege of Corfe Castle. A later Bingham was second in command of British forces in the Crimea.

There were Binghams in residence at Bingham's Melcombe from circa 1215 until 1895. Then the Bosworth Smith family arrived. It was a home on the grand scale for Rev. Reginald Bosworth Smith (1839–1908), retired master of Harrow School and rector of West Stafford, who collected avian folklore. His son, Lieutenant Alan Wyldbore Bosworth Smith, was a cool if hapless hero (1870–1901). While HMS *Cobra*, of which he was in command, was breaking up in a storm he 'remained standing on the bridge with arms folded to the last, and went down with his vessel'.

Ellinor Bosworth Smith, Reginald's daughter, married Colonel Sir Edward Ion Beresford Grogan (1873–1927) who served in the Rifle Brigade in the Boer War, followed by the Imperial Ottoman Gendarmerie in Edwardian times, and in combat with the British Army for the duration of the Great War.

Lady Grogan died in 1948 and the property was bought by the Honourable Sir Francis Hopwood, 3rd Baron Southborough (1897–1982), the managing director of Shell Petroleum. In the final years of the twentieth century it has been the home of Irene and John Langham.

Robert Worth Bingham (1871–1937), the United States Ambassador in London from 1933 until his death, traced his ancestry from here. 'I'm as British as you,' he used to tell his dinner guests. 'I am a Dorsetshire man descended from the Binghams of Bingham's Melcombe.'

So too were the fighting Binghams of the Great War and the Second World War. Notable names listed on the memorial in St Andrew's parish church include those of the 5th and 6th Earl of Lucan who were grandfather and father of Richard John Bingham (born 18 December 1934). Lord Bingham succeeded to the family's main title on his father's death in 1966, and it was as the 7th Earl of Lucan that he went 'missing' on failing to answer charges relating to the murder of his children's nanny and is now presumed dead, his remains having been allegedly fed to tigers in a private zoo.

BLOXWORTH HOUSE

Savage — Trenchard — Pickard — Pickard-Cambridge — Lane

Jacobean Bloxworth House has been immortalised as Bathsheba Everdine's residence in John Schlesinger's film of Thomas Hardy's *Far from the Madding Crowd*. An earlier manor house, which had belonged to Cerne Abbey from 987 to 1539, became home of Richard Savage in 1547. The present brick-built house is dated 1608 and was built by his descendant George Savage. After 1660 it was purchased by Sir John Trenchard (1640–95), youngest son of Thomas Trenchard of Wolfeton, who was born at Lytchett Matravers.

He was with his brother-in-law, Charles Speke, in Ilminster when news came that the Duke of Monmouth had landed at Lyme Regis in June 1685. Realising he was implicated as a potential conspirator against James II, he rode home to pack his bags for Weymouth, and exile on the continent. Speke stayed to face the consequences and was strung up and hanged outside his house.

Jacobean Bloxworth House in 1857

Friends managed to obtain a royal pardon for Trenchard in 1687 and he was elected Member of Parliament for Dorchester. He then weathered the Glorious Revolution with flying colours and was knighted by William III in 1690. By now he was sitting in Parliament for Poole and capped his career by being appointed His Majesty's Principal Secretary of State in 1692. He reformed the network of British spies in French ports and devised a complex system of numerical ciphers. This 'turbulent and aspiring politician' died in his prime and is buried just inside the entrance to the north chapel of Bloxworth parish church.

Sir John's son, George Trenchard, inherited the house. His daughter, Henrietta Trenchard, married Jocelyn Pickard of Lincoln's Inn. George Trenchard sold Bloxworth to Jocelyn Pickard. Woolsbarrow, the conspicuous flat-topped hill in the middle of the heath, used to be known as Pickard's Lookout. Bloxworth, meanwhile, became the home of rector and squire Rev. George Pickard who was required to take the additional name Cambridge in 1848 upon his succession to the property of his cousin, Charles Owen Cambridge, of Whitminster House, Gloucestershire. He was also the surviving link with the Trenchard line after its last representatives died at Wolfeton and Lytchett.

John Trenchard in residence at Bloxworth in 1790

George's fifth son, Rev. Octavius Pickard-Cambridge (1828–1917), followed in his father's spiritual footsteps, though often restricted them to the few that took him across the flower-garden in the Rectory grounds to his 'Den' out-building. Here he sorted and studied thousands of specimens of spiders. He produced the first full survey for anywhere in Britain – which became the national standard work – and then went on to produce the Arachnida of other English counties. He was working at the remarkable point in the development of a new subject that enabled him to compile the first descriptions of hundreds of species of spiders and Lepidoptera.

For eighty-one years he collected them from across the varying local country-side of Morden Park, Bloxworth Heath and Bere Wood, and made many trips to the stony island of Portland, but was always particularly pleased when a kamikaze creature was 'rash enough to appear on the window of his Den'. All 5000 specimen bottles and their multiple tubes were bequeathed to Oxford University.

Julie Christie established Bloxworth's lasting fame when it was her home, as Bathsheba Everdene, in the classic 1967 film of a Thomas Hardy novel

Remembered as 'always a boy among boys' the last little excitement of his life occurred on 8 June 1916 when he saw, for the first and only time, a flying-machine.

His sons were Colonel Robert Jocelyn Pickard-Cambridge (1867), John Trenchard Pickard-Cambridge (1869), Arthur Wallace Pickard-Cambridge (1873), Charles Owen Pickard-Cambridge (1874), Alfred Edward Lloyd Pickard-Cambridge (1876), and William Adair Pickard-Cambridge (1879). Colonel Pickard-Cambridge, who inherited Bloxworth House, bequeathed the property to his only daughter and it passed into the Lane family for most of the next century.

BRANKSEA CASTLE

Benson — Sturt — Chad — Foster — Waugh — Cavendish-Bentinck —
Balfour — van Raalte — Wheeler — Christie

Henry VIII's blockhouse at Brownsea Castle transformed into an offshore country seat, in a print of 1818

The original Branksea Castle, a blockhouse of Henry VIII's coast defences in 1547, survives in the basement of its Gothic successor on Brownsea Island, and guarded the entrance to Poole Harbour. Now owned by the National Trust, and leased as a holiday hotel to the John Lewis Partnership, it holds the Dorset record for eccentric owners.

The first, who added a 'great hall' to the fort, was William Benson (1682-1754) who moved to the island in about 1710. He published a Letter to Sir Jacob Bankes in which he argued that kings were only accountable to God. It sold 100,000 copies. He was also a wealthy sponsor of the arts, printing Samuel Johnson's *Psalms* and erecting the monument to John Milton in Westminster Abbey. Alexander Pope ridiculed him; 'On poets' tombs see Benson's titles writ.'

Frederick, Prince of Wales, was among his visitors on Brownsea Island. Benson then suffered a serious mental breakdown and his former love of books turned to hatred. He ended his days being known as 'Mad Benson'. Poole people believed he practised necromancy and that covens of witches met on the island.

Humphry Sturt (1725–86) of Crichel House bought Brownsea in 1765 and set about creating an extraordinary offshore estate. He rebuilt the castle into a

Branksea Castle (left) and the island church (right) in Philip Brannon's engraving, from Poole Harbour, in 1857

four-storey tower with side wings branching out from each corner. Thousands of trees were planted. The Sturt family eventually sold Brownsea in about 1815 to Sir Charles Chad who held it until 1840 and built cottages called Seymer's House, now in ruins, overlooking the northern shore. The entire island was turned into parkland with the planting of the trees.

Sir Augustus John Foster (1780–1848), a diplomat, was sent to Washington as Minister Plenipotentiary. He failed to sort out a simmering row over the impressment of American sailors into the Royal Navy which began in 1807. Matters came to a head in June 1812. Without anyone across the Atlantic realising that London had backed down on the 16th, and cancelled the contentious orders, the Americans declared war on the 18th and prepared to invade Canada. That offensive was outmanoeuvred and British troops came south to burn the Capitol in 1813 and destroy most of the Library of Congress. The great American victory, at New Orleans, did not take place until 1815.

Foster had won his place in history, as the last man to put us at war with the United States of America, and was given postings of little consequence, to Copenhagen and Turin. On retirement in 1840 he bought Brownsea but far from finding an island paradise he fell into bouts of deep depression, ending his life by slitting his throat in Branksea Castle in 1848.

Colonel William Petrie Waugh bought the island for £13,000 in 1852. As director of the London and Eastern Banking Corporation he had no difficulty raising £237,000 after a geologist told him 'a most valuable bed of the finest clay' was worth 'at least £10,000 an acre'. As well as building Branksea Pottery he restored and embellished the castle, spent £10,000 on building a church, and drained St Andrew's Bay. The pottery failed to live up to expectations and the bank in London tottered on the brink of insolvency. Shareholders asked Waugh to repay the loan, in 1857, and he fled to Spain.

Tea party at Branksea Castle given by Charles and Florence van Raalte for the island staff

Charles van Raalte promoting his candidature for the East Dorset constituency

Brownsea in bankruptcy failed to realise its £50,000 reserve. It was eventually sold to George Augustus Frederick Cavendish-Bentinck (1821–91), for £30,000 in 1870. He brought numerous art objects to the island and was buried beneath an elegant Italian marble pozzo dating from 1497.

The next owner, Lieutenant-Colonel Kenneth Robert Balfour MP (1863–1936), watched helplessly on the night of 26 January 1896 as Branksea Castle was gutted by fire. Restoration in 1897 softened its lines by removing some of the turrets and other Gothic touches.

Wealthy socialite Charles van Raalte (1857–1907) arrived in 1901 and changed the island's name to Brownsea in 1903, after guests kept getting out of the train at Branksome by mistake. The visitor who will be remembered longest was Robert Baden-Powell, with 20 boys, between 1–9 August 1907. They pitched the world's first Scout camp, above the old Branksea Pottery, and started a worldwide youth movement.

An era ended with Florence van Raalte's death, when a 2714-lot country-house sale over nine days in June 1927 raised £22,300. New owner and house clearer Sir Arthur Wheeler (1860–1943) 'decided, in view of probable developments on the island, to dismantle the castle'. In the event it was saved by the slump and sold to Mrs Mary Florence Bonham Christie (1864–1961). She depopulated the island and ceased gardening, allowing it to return to nature, and kept visitors at bay.

Five hundred Scouts were allowed to celebrate their silver jubilee in 1932. All public access came to an end after fire swept across the island in 1934. It would have destroyed the buildings at the eastern end if the wind had not changed direction just in time.

The tomb of socialite Charles van Raalte (1857–1907) in St Mary's Church on Brownsea Island

The island's history of eccentricity ended with Mrs Christie's death, in her ninety-eighth year, on 28 April 1961. Her grandson, John Bonham Christie, presented the island to the Treasury in lieu of death duties and the Government handed it to the National Trust in 1962.

BRIDEHEAD

Mellor — Bridge — Williams

The estate village of Littlebredy, deep in a chalkland fold between Dorchester and Bridport, is one of the prettiest in Dorset. Overlooking the scene is a Christmas-cake church of Victorian Gothic. House, community and parish church all have medieval origins but they were transformed into a coherent entity in 1850 by Christchurch-born architect Benjamin Ferry.

'Briddy' as it is locally known, derives from a Celtic word for 'boil' which applied to the spring that was a conspicuous feature until inundation by a Victorian lake. Littlebredy's recorded history starts as the Saxon manor of Brydian which was owned by Cerne Abbey. In 1600 it was the home of Sir Robert Mellor who built a manor house on the site of the present mansion. Then the Bridge family were in residence until the arrival of the Williams clan in 1797.

Benjamin Ferry was commissioned to turn Littlebredy into a 'model village' by City banker Robert Williams (1811–90), the leading partner at Williams and Deacon's Bank, who also enhanced the landscape by damming the source of the River Bride to create a lake. Williams then gave the place a magic name. He coined 'Bridehead' for his revamped country seat.

The Williams link with 3000 acres of this downland landscape came with an earlier Robert Williams (1734–1814) of Moor Park, Hertford who married Jane

Bridehead for revisiting, on canvas, in the 1960s

Chassereau (1739–1841). Born in Niort, she was the youngest daughter of an exiled French Protestant, Francis Chassereau, who fled to Britain after Louis XIV revoked the edict of Nantes, from 1685, thereby withdrawing freedom for non-Catholic worship. Jane's life is detailed on a memorial tablet: 'She died on the 8th of October 1841, at the age of 102 years, the mother, grand-mother, and great-grand-mother of a numerous family' having retained 'childlike cheerfulness' throughout that long life.

William Williams (died 1839), of Castle Hill, was 'for many years MP for Weymouth and Provincial Grand Master of the Ancient Society of Free and Accepted Masons for the County of Dorset'.

The next Robert Williams (1767–1847) in residence at Bridehead was the father of the rebuilding Robert Williams. His son, Colonel Sir Robert Williams (1848–1943), not only kept the banking business on the rails but was a Commissioner of Lieutenancy of the City of London and honorary Colonel of the 4th Battalion, the Dorsetshire Regiment. He married Rosa Walker Simes and was created a baronet in 1915.

Their son, Sir Philip Francis Cunningham Williams (1884–1958), was the second baronet. He married Margaret Peek, daughter of Sir Cuthbert and Lady Peek, and was High Sheriff of Dorset in 1949.

Son and heir Sir David Philip Williams (1909–1970) married Kathleen Mary Walker who died in 1945. His second marriage was to Elizabeth Mary Garneys Bond, the daughter of Tyneham's last owner, Ralph Bond, who was then living in exile at Moigne Combe, near Crossways.

The title went to their son, and returned to a familiar name as the fourth baronet, though Sir Robert Philip Nathaniel Williams (born 1950), uses Philip instead. He married Catherine Margaret Godwin, the daughter of Canon Cosmo Pouncey of Tewkesbury, in 1979.

BRYANSTON HOUSE

Rogers — Seymour — Portman — Berkeley Portman

The Rogers family held Bryanston in the Middle Ages. Honora Rogers, the daughter of Sir Richard Rogers, married Edward Seymour, Lord Beauchamp (1561–1612) and their third son was Francis Seymour, 1st Baron Seymour of Trowbridge (1590–1664). Francis Seymour survived allegations of collaboration in the escape of his brother, William Seymour, with Arabella Stuart, and had a crucial role in numerous political intrigues, in a career that ended with the Royalist surrender of Oxford on 22 June 1645. John Aubrey spent Christmas with him at what is now Marlborough College, in 1648, and was told of Sir John Rocklington in the time of Henry VIII:

'He had a fair estate, and no child; and there was a poor cottager whose name was Rogers that had a pretty wife whom this knight did visit and had a mind to have a child by her. As he did suppose, he afterwards had; and in consideration of affection, etc, settled his whole estate on this young Rogers. William Seymour, 2nd Earl and 1st Marquess of Hertford (Duke of Somerset), was son of the grand-daughter of this Rogers.'

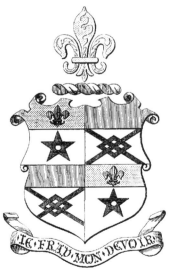

Arms of the Rogers family, Bryanston's medieval owners

The Portmans became the next and last Bryanston family when Sir William Portman (1644–90) bought the Bryanston estate and its country house in 1660. Its wooded ridge above the River Stour, between Blandford and Durweston, was on the edge of national events in July 1685. The sequel to the last battle on English soil, following the defeat of a rebel army at Sedgemoor on the Somerset Levels, came with the capture by Sir William Portman of the fugitive Duke of Monmouth in a ditch beside Horton Heath. The 'wanabee' monarch had been attempting to flee to France but instead ended up in the Tower of London where his uncle, King James II, took his head.

The family's main seat remained at Orchard Portman, between Taunton and the Blackdown Hills, and Sir William sat in Parliament for Taunton, from 1661–79, and then for Somerset until 1681, and for Taunton again from 1685 until his death. Orchard Portman was regarded as a sick old house. Sir William had lost three wives there, the servants were always going down with fevers, and it was eventually razed to the ground.

In 1688 Sir William Portman became a convert to the cause of overthrowing the Stuart throne, and led the first large-scale defection of English troops to join the invading Dutch forces of Prince William of Orange as they marched from Brixham to Exeter. James II was losing his throne to William III.

The Portman succession was equally problematic. Sir William had married three times but failed to sire an heir. Instead the Bryanston estate passed to his nephew, Henry Seymour, who assumed the name and arms of Portman. On Henry's death the Bryanston estate went to William Berkeley and the subsequent history of the Portman family was through the Berkeley-Portman succession (not that they use the hyphen). William Berkeley, from Pylle, Somerset, married Anne Seymour, the daughter of Sir Edward Seymour. He was a younger member of a branch of the family that gave its name to Berkeley Castle, Gloucestershire, and claimed Portman blood from a century earlier, tracing his pedigree back to Joan Portman, the youngest daughter of Sir John Portman, the first baronet. So he too adopted the arms and name of Portman, by Act of Parliament, in 1736. He died the following year and his son, Henry William Berkeley Portman, married Anne Fitch. He died in 1761.

Their son, Henry William Portman, married Ann Wyndham and had Bryanston House rebuilt by eminent architect James Wyatt in 1778, having

Sir William Portman (died 1555) was Lord Chief Justice of England

Sir William Portman (1644-89), the last baronet at Bryanston, who captured the rebel Duke of Monmouth

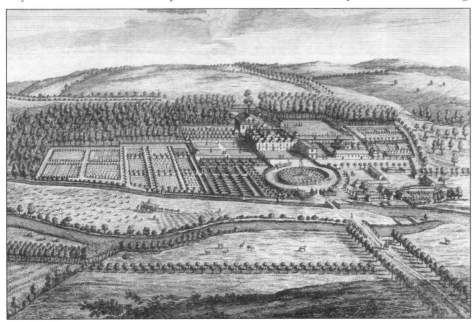

Bryanston House was surrounded by formal gardens in the 18th century

Thomas Gainsborough's portrait of Henry William Berkeley Portman (died 1761)

Edward Berkeley Portman MP (died 1823) was the father of the 1st Viscount Portman

bought High Hall, near Wimborne, as a second home. He built Durweston Bridge to move the road from the village to Blandford, out of his park, and with it the principal route into the Blackmore Vale. Henry Portman also developed the principal source of the family's wealth, with bricks and mortar across its Marylebone fields. Buildings now spread to its extremities, beside and beyond the new Marylebone Road – London's first relief road – which by-passed Oxford Street and its crush of cattle being driven into the capital. Henry William Portman joined his father in the vault in St Martin's Church, Bryanston in 1796.

The next son and heir was Edward Berkeley Portman MP (1771–1823) who married clergyman's daughter Lucy Whitby. In 1806 he wrestled one of the two Dorset county seats from the Bankes family, and held it for the rest of his life, dying on Parliamentary business in Rome.

The family status was lifted by son Edward Berkeley Portman MP (1799–1888) who was persuaded to stand against Bankes, for the seat in the House of Commons, in the election of 1823 during which year his father had died. He showed much more enthusiasm in establishing the Portman Hunt and became the family's first noble lord, being created Baron Portman of Orchard Portman (in 1837) and then Viscount Portman of Bryanston (in 1873). His expertise in cattle breeding at Websley Farm, Durweston, resulted in the Devon breed – which was soon being exported to the plains of South Africa and Uruguay – and brought him the presidency of the Royal Agricultural Society, of which he was a founder member.

In 1827 he married Lady Emma Lascelles, third daughter of the Earl of Harewood, who was chosen by the new Queen Victoria, in 1837, as one of her Ladies of the Bedchamber. She attended Queen Victoria at her coronation and was Matron of Honour at her wedding to Prince Albert. Edward also served the Crown as a Councillor of the Duchy of Cornwall and the Duchy of Lancaster.

Lord Portman's son and heir William Henry Berkeley, 2nd Viscount Portman (1829-1919), had a decisive sense of place and purpose which he displayed in the political and hunting fields and on the lasting canvas of the local landscape. Having sat as a Whig in the House of Commons from 1852 to 1885 he departed with the 8th Duke of Devonshire in protest at the party's conversion to the cause of Home Rule for Ireland.

From then on he preferred devoting his personal energies to the Portman Hunt but spending too much time in Dorset made him consider whether to flatten the ancestral home. Mary, his wife, cited damp and other discomforts as the reason for 'needing a new house for a new century'. It has been pointed out that it was also relevant that Lady Portman, the only child of Viscount Milton, the heir to Earl Fitzwilliam, had been born in an ancestral home without equal; 'Wentworth Woodhouse, in Yorkshire, was the largest private house in England.'

On succeeding his father, he immediately set about leaving a permanent mark on the landscape by replacing the family's characterful Wyatt house with a visually disconcerting red-brick slab designed to enormous proportions by Norman Shaw. He was definitely an urban architect, who has left his mark beside the Thames, where his best known building is New Scotland Yard. The site of the old stately home is under the grass beside the church and is haunted by the ghost of the White Lady. She was identified by the family historian, Marjorie Portman, as Charlotte Fanny, the daughter of Edward Berkeley Portman's Uncle Henry, who always wanted to inherit the house she loved so much. ''Tis only Cousin Charlotte, not to worry,' Edward reassured his nurse in old age. The new Bryanston House was completed in 1890.

William Henry Berkeley married the Honourable Mary Selina Wentworth-Fitzwilliam, daughter of Viscount Milton, and they had many sons. However, a series of relatively early deaths shifted the title sideways rather than onwards, and a double whammy of death duties during the Depression caused the loss of Bryanston House, though the family sensibly retained ownership of the Marylebone estate in central London and remained one of the richest families in the land. The two crucial deaths were those of Henry Berkeley, 3rd Viscount Portman (1860–1923), and his brother Claud Berkeley, 4th Viscount Portman (1864–1929). The latter had one daughter from his first marriage, which ended when his wife divorced him in 1897, and a son and two daughters from his second liaison. The son was Edward Claud Berkeley, 5th Viscount Portman (1899–1942) whose marriage only produced daughters.

The succession therefore went back a generation to Seymour Berkeley, 6th Viscount Portman (1868–1946), the eldest surviving son of the 2nd Viscount. On his death the title went to Gerald Berkeley, 7th Viscount Portman (1875–1948), before breaking out of the nineteenth century and moving on to his son, Gerald William Berkeley, 8th Viscount Portman (1903–1967) and his nephew Edward Henry Berkeley, 9th Viscount Portman (born 1934).

The 2nd Viscount Portman (1829–1919) of Bryanston House

Gerald was always particularly proud of having been the only member of the family to have been born in its London residence, at 22 Portman Square, which had been home to the socialite Mrs Elizabeth Montagu who hosted the first 'blue-stocking' conversation parties. In Dorset there were still Portman descendants beside their former Bryanston parkland, at Durweston, but the title had left the county. Their home, so excellently barrack-built by Norman Shaw, passed to the Crown Commissioners in lieu of death duties in 1929 and had its reincarnation as Bryanston School, housing 600 pupils and staff.

The Portman family gathered around the 2nd Viscount in the Drawing Room, Bryanston House, about 1900

CAME HOUSE

Damer — Martin

Came House, engraved in 1794, when it was the seat of the Honourable Lionel Damer

The magnificent Palladian mansion in the next valley south-east from Dorchester was built in 1754 by John Damer, a younger brother of Joseph Damer who was busy in mid-Dorset with the transformation of Middleton town and Milton Abbey. It was the main work of provincial architect Francis Cartwright of Blandford St Mary. The elder Damer brother was created Lord Milton and then the 1st Earl of Dorchester.

Lord Dorchester's son, the Honourable Lionel Damer, married Williamsa, niece of Sir Theodore Janssen, in 1778. They resided at Came and regularly entertained King George III and his Queen on their visits to Weymouth.

Mary Georgiana Seymour was the second daughter of Admiral Lord Hugh Seymour, son of the 1st Marquess of Hertford, and Anne Horatia, the daughter of James, 2nd Earl Waldegrave. In 1825, Mary Seymour married Colonel the Right Honourable George Lionel Dawson Damer, a Privy Councillor, who was the third son of the 1st Earl Portarlington. They were bequeathed Came House on the death of Lady Caroline Damer, daughter of the 1st Earl of Dorchester from Milton Abbey, in 1828.

In 1847, Georgiana Dawson Damer, the eldest daughter of Colonel and Mrs Dawson Damer, married Viscount Ebrington, later Earl Fortescue. Prince Louis Napoleon, afterwards Emperor of the French, was visiting Came House and attended the wedding. He signed the register as a witness. Then James Frampton of Moreton House added his signature – at the age of seventy-eight – 'as being the oldest friend of the family, as well as the oldest person present'.

From the Damers the house descended to Captain William Frederick Martin and Lady Christian Martin (died 1959).

Came House in 1905

CANFORD HOUSE

Salisbury — Beaufort — Courtenay — Blount —
Ponsonby — de Mauley — Guest — Wimborne

Plantagenet-period owners at Canford were the Earls of Salisbury, followed by the Beaufort, Courtenay and Blount families. Though its ancient hall was known as John of Gaunt's Kitchen, the manor at Canford did not come into the property portfolio of the Duchy of Lancaster until after John's lifetime. Most of the medieval building was demolished in 1765 and Canford's great revival began in the following century after purchase by Poole MP William Ponsonby, 1st Baron de Mauley. Its rebuilding by architect Edward Blore, whose south front survives, took place in 1826. Ponsonby's peerage was created in 1838.

That year a baronetcy was bestowed on one of Britain's leading industrialists. Sir Josiah John Guest MP (1785–1852) owned Dowlais Ironworks, Merthyr Tydfil, which produced rails for the railways. He invented the blast-furnace. Largely for the benefit of his health, he ploughed £350,000 of his profits into buying Canford Manor and its thousands of acres in 1846. The estate ran from Wimborne to the sea where it gave its name to Canford Cliffs. Guest had the house enlarged by Sir Charles Barry who was at the time also rebuilding the Houses of Parliament.

Sir Josiah resented time spent in the Dorset countryside and continually returned to Wales, refusing to relinquish control of his great firm, on which the livelihood of 12,000 families depended. He took an active interest in civil engineering and was chairman of the Taff Valley railway. His final return enabled him to die amid his beloved industries; his monument is in Dowlais church.

In 1833, Guest married Charlotte Elizabeth Bertie (1812–95), the daughter of the 9th Earl of Lindsey, who gave him ten children during the next thirteen years. She also found time to be one of the great Welsh scholars of all time, translating the medieval manuscripts that formed the *Mabinogion*, published between 1838 and 1849. These provided her friend, Alfred Tennyson, with the Arthurian legends that formed the basis for his *Idylls of the King* in 1859.

Charlotte's second marriage was to Charles Schreiber, in 1855, which ended with his death in 1884. She also made a major impact upon British culture by one of her 'good works'. This was a shelter for London cabmen which was kept supplied with newspapers and thereby helped to create one of the most

Charlotte Guest, Welsh scholar, who presented collections to the nation

'Canford Manor and Lady Wimborne' in an Edwardian postcard which showed where power lay

articulate and opinionated groups in the land. Her porcelain collection was presented to the Victoria and Albert Museum in memory of her second husband, Charles. She then published two lavish volumes on her collection of painted fans which were given to the British Museum in 1891.

Her third son and veteran of the Indian Mutiny, Montague Guest (1839–1909) went into politics. He was Liberal MP for Youghal, from 1869 to 1874, and then represented Wareham from 1880 to 1885 when he became Liberal-Unionist. He was Provincial Grand Master for Dorsetshire, appointed by His Royal Highness Albert Edward, Prince of Wales. There his connection extended beyond Freemasonry to close friendship. Monty Guest died whilst visiting him, now King Edward VII, at Sandringham for the King's birthday party on 9 November 1909.

The heyday of the great mansion at Canford Magna, between Poole and Wimborne, began in style when the eldest son, Sir Ivor Guest (1835-1914), came of age in August 1858 and took over the estate. A series of parties lasted for eighteen hours. The events began for 800 children and progressed to a ball for 800 members of county and national society which went on through to a huge fireworks display and continued all night. It did not end until 'God Save the Queen' was played at 6 o'clock in the morning.

Sir Ivor knew how to party but was a disappointment in politics. He failed in four attempts to enter the House of Commons and was spared further embarrassment by being created Baron Wimborne, by Disraeli, in 1880.

Cornelia, Lady Wimborne, aunt of Winston Churchill, headed a family of aspiring politicians

The key character in the Canford story – the family's driving force – was not Lord Wimborne but Lady Wimborne. In 1868, Ivor Guest married Lady Cornelia Spencer-Churchill (1847–1927). Her famous brother was the statesman of high Toryism, Lord Randolph Churchill (1849–95), the founder of the Primrose League, who on 12 August 1885 was the guest speaker – deliberate pun – as some 3000 people swarmed across Canford's spacious lawns for the Great Conservative Fête. Lord Wimborne, in his words of welcome, said it was gratifying to see so many ladies in pink. This had been chosen for Churchill's colours at his recent Woodstock election. Lord Randolph then gave a resounding speech. He assured the gathering that whatever the *Daily News* might suggest he was not trying to make war with Russia over control of the Indian sub-continent.

'Well that journal has always held me up as being an incompetent idiot,' he said. 'Quite right,' someone shouted. 'The accusation comes to this,' Lord Randolph continued, 'that I would gladly rick, would gladly sacrifice the lives of 250,000 human beings in order what for? To gain a few thousand Conservative votes at the General Election!' The speech gathered force as a rendition of what he saw as 'the substance of Tory realities to the illusion of Radical policies'.

By 1901 there was another Churchill in Parliament. Winston Spencer Churchill was the son of Lord Randolph Churchill. The Guest family at Canford had become Liberals and Aunt Cornelia – Lady Wimborne – was in the gallery of the House of Commons to hear young Winston's maiden speech on 18 February 1901. She was the strong woman behind the rising star.

In 1906, Winston was Colonial Under-Secretary in the Campbell-Bannerman administration and Lady Wimborne picked up the tab for him to entertain ministers from all the territories of the British Empire at a dinner in the Ritz Hotel. She opposed High-Church ceremonies in the Church of England, denouncing them as 'Rome-ish', and founded Cornelia's League of Ladies which had 40 branches across the country. Frederick Smith, later created Earl of Birkenhead, was one of her paid secretaries. He decorated his office with a few religious pictures. 'Rome-ish,' Lady Wimborne raged when she heard about them. She dismissed him with immediate effect.

Winston nearly ended his life before his career had started at the Guests' seaside villa at Canford Cliffs. What the family modestly described as their 'Beach House' was a palatial mansion known as Branksome Dene. Eighteen-year-old Winston had fallen 20 feet from the rustic bridge that used to cross nearby Alum Chine whilst playing with fourteen-year-old cousin, Ivor Churchill Guest (1873–1939). It happened in 1892 and Winston lay comatose for three days at Branksome Dene. It was more than three months before his ruptured kidney healed sufficiently for him to leave his sick-bed. Convalescence followed at Canford House.

Winston was still enjoying the company of Ivor in 1906. A Liberal rally was held at Canford on August Bank Holiday and Ivor – who had also taken part in the South African War – presided as 15,000 people strained to hear the Under-Secretary of State for the Colonies speak at great length about most of the problems of the day. In South Africa, as a colonial possession, the difficulty was that winning the Boer War had not been enough in itself to ensure English ascendancy. The majority of settlers were of Dutch origin. Churchill advocated a solution of divide and rule, by vigorously and skilfully promoting self-government, for the Transvaal and Orange River Colony.

Young Winston: Lord Randolph's son was the protégé of aunt Cornelia at Canford House

On Saturday 31 July 1909, Winston was again staying at Canford and visited the corner of the Guest estate that was being suburbanised as a dormitory for Poole and Bournemouth artisans. He opened the Branksome Liberal Club during celebrations that were interrupted by suffragette protests. Winston was then President of the Board of Trade and had just spiked the miners' intended strike. Lady Wimborne had provided an acre of land for the Branksome Club and had insisted that it provided separate accommodation exclusively for women. 'We don't want a room, we want a vote!' they chanted.

The ladies returned in strength to hear Winston address the Radical Fête and Demonstration at Canford House on the Bank Holiday Monday in August 1909. Mrs Emmeline Pankhurst and her daughters led the protests and had to be protected by the police. Canford employed 221 under-gardeners and at least another hundred healthy outdoor males, who had gathered as an army and were about to throw a cordon of pig-nets around the women, as a prelude to ducking them in the River Stour.

Winston's father: Lord Randolph Churchill addressed the Great Conservative Fête at Canford in 1885

Winston had a Liberal budget to defend and memories of his father's great speech to live down. That was twenty-four years before, when Lord and Lady Wimborne were stalwart Conservatives, and when Lord Randolph Churchill hammered into the Liberal radicalism that Churchill and Lady Wimborne now extolled. Winston was irritated by the suffragette interruptions.

In 1910, Lady Wimborne went too far, even for Lady Wimborne. In ensuring the election to Parliament of her third son, 'Freddie' Guest (1875–1937), the rules restricting expenditure and against treating had been openly violated. Votes in the East Dorset constituency had been bought, an election court declared, as it ruled Freddie's votes void. In the resulting by-election the family's substitute, elder brother Henry Guest (1874–1957), was duly elected. Then the country went to the polls for the second General Election of 1910 and in East Dorset's third count of the year Captain Freddie Guest was back on the ballot paper. Winston returned to do his bit on the hustings in Poole and Guest's daughters were sent out through the streets in a cart decked out with

'Vote for Daddy' with young members of the Guest family showing that the photo-call is nothing new

the slogan: 'Vote for Daddy'. Freddie won, of course, against Brigadier-General John Nicholson.

This nepotism extended to Winston himself. He tried to push Freddie's virtues on a reluctant Asquith, trying to have him made Civil Lord of the Admiralty, but the Prime Minister rejected all suggestions. Freddie Guest became aide-de-camp to Field Marshal Sir John French, who commanded the British Expeditionary Force in France, but failed to save his boss from Lord Kitchener's wrath as the butcher's bill mounted on the Western Front.

In 1917 Freddie Guest became Lloyd George's Chief Whip and was at last in a position to do Winston a favour. He had lost the Admiralty, as a result of the debacle in the Dardanelles, with the failure of the Gallipoli landings. Eventually, and partly due to Freddie's insistence, he was back in Government as Minister of Munitions.

Like mother, like son. Freddie was soon caught up in the scandal which followed revelations that Lloyd George's administration was selling peerages and other honours. Cornelia had always told Freddie that everyone had their price and it never occurred to him that there might be anything dubious about the system. Then he tried to make alliances with just about anyone and everyone who had a vote in the House of Commons. Coalitions were variously suggested with the Tories, Unionists, Asquith's faction of the split Liberal Party, and failing all else the Labour Party. Because the press could no longer take this seriously, Freddie and a few friends decided to acquire their own national newspaper, and bought the *Daily Chronicle* to provide themselves with a platform.

'East Dorset Speaks' with Lady Wimborne flanked by sons Ivor and Freddie Guest

In 1921, Freddie moved into Winston's seat as Secretary of State for Air, when Winston climbed another rung of the ministerial ladder and became Colonial Secretary. Here, at least, Freddie was as qualified as anyone in Westminster. He not only enjoyed flying, and held a pilot's licence, but also owned his own airfield. Moortown Aerodrome was on the edge of Canford village. It was his passion and he was actively involved in aviation for the rest of his life. After giving up the country's air portfolio he became Squadron Leader the Right Honourable Frederick E. Guest PC, CBE, DSO, MP. He flew an Avro DH9a when serving in the Auxiliary Air Force with No. 600 (City of London) Bombing Squadron.

By 1935 both Winston and Freddie had crossed the political fence and were returned as Conservatives. Freddie's seat was Plymouth's Drake division. His eldest brother, Ivor, had meanwhile come and gone from the political scene, taking high office as Paymaster General in 1910 and succeeding their father as 2nd Baron Wimborne in 1914, and making an exit from national affairs at the end of the decade as His Majesty's Lord Lieutenant in troubled Ireland which was about to face partition and civil war. In recognition he was elevated to be 1st Viscount Wimborne. On the home front he was acceptable to both sides as a mediator between the National Government and the Labour Party in the negotiations to end the General Strike in 1926.

As her sons reached and passed their peaks, Lady Wimborne gradually relaxed her political and territorial grasp. 'How about emigration?' is said to have been her stock phrase for solving the problems of the Depression. She sold Canford House in 1923 and it became a public school. For the final four years of her life she lived in the next country seat up the Stour valley, in Merley House, to the south of Wimborne. No one under-estimated them during the time they were around, except for poor Ivor whose mediocrity was immortalised by Hilaire Belloc:

> Grant, O Lord, eternal rest
> to thy servant Ivor Guest.
> Never mind the where or how
> Only grant it to him now.

CHANTMARLE

Cheverell — Oglander — Savile — Hornby

The original owners of Chantmarle, in the upper Frome valley a mile north of Cattistock, were the Cheverell family. They were the residents from the time of Henry VI until 1606 when Christopher Cheverell borrowed heavily against the property and defaulted on his mortgages. The opportunity was seized by lawyer Sir John Strode of Parnham House.

He commissioned architect Gabriel Moore, from Chinnock, near Yeovil, to build a new Chantmarle. Strode and Moore chose golden yellow stone from Ham Hill, in sight of Chinnock, and their masons, from the quarries above Stoke-sub-Hamdon, were Joseph and Daniel Rowe. The imposing three-storey porch carries 1612 as the completion date. The cost had been £1142 and only a part of one wing, off at an angle from the back, was retained from the original house. This appears to have been spared because it contained an ancient chapel. Strode also provided himself with a replacement private chapel though the latter was demolished in the nineteenth century.

By this time, as with Parnham, Chantmarle had descended to the Oglanders and was effectively de-gentrified into a farmhouse. Francis Ewart Savile bought it in 1910 and proceeded to reverse years of neglect. The barrister Charles Harry St John Hornby (1867–1946) arrived in 1919 and concentrated on doing much the same for the gardens. He was the director of W.H. Smith & Son, and a trustee of the Wallace Collection, from 1933, and the British Museum from 1936.

In 1950 Chantmarle was acquired by the Ministry of Works and passed to the Home Office for a Police Training Centre.

CHARBOROUGH PARK

Erle — Drax — Sawbridge Erle Drax — Plunkett-Ernle-Erle-Drax

Only one successful revolution was plotted in Dorset. The unsuccessful sort were often in provincial hearts and minds, as with the hopes that landed at Lyme Regis in the summer of 1685, when the Duke of Monmouth attempted to seize the Stuart crown from his uncle, James II. Meanwhile another contender waited on the other side of the North Sea and learned from the slaughter of Dorset and Somerset's politically naive peasants.

William, Prince of Orange-Nassau, in the cultural heart of the Netherlands, planned something more sophisticated to unseat his uncle. William was married to Mary, the daughter of James II, which gave an interest and legitimacy to what would become their joint claim upon the English throne. That it was ever there for the taking was due not so much to James's imposition of tyrannical rule as to the fact that his open reintroduction of Catholicism was totally unacceptable to the majority of the English people.

William's was to be an elitist rather than a popular uprising. It would belong to the Europe of the post Middle Ages where an intellectual grasp of power had to underwrite any reversal of the status quo. Here, in the political colour code, it would be a blue revolution quietly manoeuvred by the gentry rather than the impetuous mass movement of the country people that had literally turned red as a disciplined national army cut it to the core at Sedgemoor.

The wealthy landed aristocracy were more cautious and exercised similar care over whom they would next entrust with power over their heads. So it was in 1688 that the shape of British constitutional politics for the rest of the millennium was plotted in the ice-house on the rise just above Charborough House in wooded countryside five miles north-west of Poole. It has a fine marble inscription, set into the bank above the door by Thomas Erle Drax in 1780, which tells the story with vigour and passion:

> Under this roof in the year MDCLXXXVI
> a set of patriotic gentlemen
> of this neighbourhood
> concerted the great plan
> of THE GLORIOUS REVOLUTION
> with THE IMMORTAL KING WILLIAM
> to whom we owe our deliverance
> from Popery and Slavery
> the expansion of our Liberties
> security of our Properties
> and establishment of National Honor and Wealth.
> ENGLISHMEN remember this glorious era
> and consider that your liberties procured
> by the virtue of your ancestors
> must be maintained by yourselves.

Thomas Erle was the landowner who gave a secure roof to the cause. The commemorative stone was cut by a proud descendant: 'Thomas Erle Drax erected this stone in the year MDCCLXXX.'

Their revolution came to pass in the West Country when at noon on Monday 5 November 1688 a Dutch fleet dropped anchor in Tor Bay. Eighteen guns covered the Prince of Orange as his barge came as close as it could at low tide

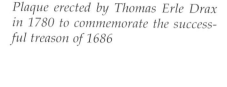

Plaque erected by Thomas Erle Drax in 1780 to commemorate the successful treason of 1686

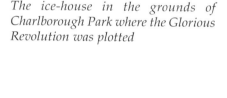

The ice-house in the grounds of Charlborough Park where the Glorious Revolution was plotted

to the shore at Brixham. William shouted a welcome to the crowd that had gathered to receive him, though his broken English contained a delightful double entendre: 'Mine good people, I am come for your goods. I am come for all your goods.'

His standard showed the arms of Nassau quartered with England's, representing William's marriage to Mary, which now took on a territorial dimension. His motto pledged: 'Liberate et religion je meintiendray' (I will uphold liberty and religion). What unfolded was an almost regal progress towards the Court of St James which by that time was vacant as King James had fled on a boat to France.

General Thomas Erle (1650–1720) had sat for Wareham in the House of Commons from 1678 and was appointed Deputy Lieutenant for Dorset in 1685. In the absence of the Lord Lieutenant, Lord Bristol, he was responsible with Colonel Strangways and Sir Henry Portman in organising mobilisation of the Red Regiment of the Dorset Militia to enter Bridport and prevent the eastwards movement of Monmouth's rebels. On 8 March 1689, no longer propping up an unpopular king, Major Thomas Erle was appointed Colonel of a newly formed Regiment of Foot which he took to Ireland and commanded through a series of actions against the defiant rump of James's Army. The Battle of the Boyne, on 1 July 1690, was followed by the Siege of Limerick and a campaign across the bogs in 1691 which culminated in the Battle of Aghrim. In the course of the fight, which was eventually won, Colonels Erle and Herbert were taken prisoner and the former was lucky not to share the fate of the latter, who was 'barbarously murdered by the Irish, when they saw he was likely to be rescued'.

The pagoda-like Charborough Tower which Thomas Hardy immortalised in Two on a Tower

Erle's next command was of Francis Luttrell's Regiment, the 19th Foot, which he took to Flanders and led at the Battle of Steinkirk on 3 August 1692. He remained their Colonel until 1709 and was promoted to Brigadier-General on 22 March 1693, in time for the Battle of Landen, where he was badly wounded.

He recovered and provided supporting forces at the Siege of Namur. Luttrell's Regiment of Foot evolved into the Green Howards.

In 1699, Major-General Erle was appointed deputy to Lord Galway in Ireland, becoming Commander-in-Chief on the accession of Queen Anne. In 1703, as Lieutenant-General Erle, Lieutenant of the Ordnance, he returned to England and raised a Regiment of Dragoons which was sent to Ireland under the command of Lord Cutts. Erle then served under Lord Rivers and went to Spain as part of the Allied expedition under Lord Galway. Against over-whelming odds, wounded in an action in which many of his men were killed, he was forced to retreat from the Battle of Almanza in which the French (under the command of an Englishman, the Duke of Berwick) were victorious. Back at Charborough, in 1718, he commissioned Sir James Thornhill to decorate the magnificent Painted Hall.

His only daughter, Frances, married Sir Edward Ernley of Maddington, Wiltshire, and their daughter and heir, Frances-Elizabeth Ernley, married Henry Drax of Ellerton Abbey, Swaledale. The Drax name had transferred to Dorset though it remains larger than ever in Yorkshire as a result of Drax Power Station. Drax is a village ten miles from Selby.

Henry Drax was the secretary of Frederick, Prince of Wales, and added a new wing to Charborough in anticipation of a royal visit in 1741. When the Prince died a decade later he was the subject of the ultimate ditty:

Here lies Fred,
who was alive and is dead.
Had it been his father
I had much rather.
Had it been his brother,
still better than the other.
Had it been his sister,
no one would have missed her.
Had it been the whole generation,
all the better for the nation.
But since 'tis only Fred,
that was alive and is dead,
Why, there's no more to be said.

The wealth of the Drax family and Charborough came from seventeenth-century sugar plantations and the associated rum trade in Jamaica and Barbados. Colonel Sir James Drax pioneered the industry, from before 1638, and was said 'to have lived like a prince'. There were Drax Hall Plantations on both islands. In Barbados the family would continue to own Drax Hall and Drax Hope for the rest of the millennium. East of Cardiff Hall, the property includes Don Christopher's Cove, where Christopher Columbus beached for a year on his fourth and last voyage to the New World. Slavery and penal trans-portation provided the labour for the West Indies colonies and the family's inventory and accounts for 1805 show a figure of 205 slaves in their ownership in Barbados at the end of the year, during which one or two had died and another nine children were born.

Thomas Erle-Drax owned Charborough from 1755 to 1790. In 1765 he expanded the Morden estates further east with the acquisition of former Turberville lands, from the Tregonwell family, at Abbot's Court, Winterborne Kingston. More followed including the core of the bulk of the historic estate around Bere Regis and the Jacobean Woolbridge Manor which was immor-talised by Thomas Hardy, for the momentary honeymoon of Tess of the

The arms of Sawbridge-Erle-Drax

Eccentric squire John Samuel Wanley Sawbridge Erle Drax (1800-87) setting off from Charborough Park

d'Urbervilles. The Drax succession briefly passed to brother Edward Drax who had married Mary Churchill from nearby Henbury, Sturminster Marshall. Their daughter, Sarah Frances, married Richard Grosvenor MP who assumed the name Erle-Drax-Grosvenor.

The next daughter and heir, Jane-Frances Erle-Drax-Grosvenor, married John Samuel Wanley Sawbridge (1800–87), shortly before she inherited Charborough Park at Morden and similar large estates in Wiltshire, Yorkshire, Wimbledon and Barbados. Sawbridge came to Charborough on 23 August 1828 and thereafter called himself John Samuel Wanley Sawbridge Erle Drax and founded the Charborough Hunt. His 60-feet parkland pagoda was struck by lightning on 29 November 1838 and was replaced by the 120-feet Charborough Tower, which has 161 steps, in 1839. He sat for Wareham in the House of Commons for nearly half a century, the seat having been saved by a timely manoeuvre from Reform Act disfranchisement, but infuriated his friends by changing allegiance from Whig to Tory. He is said to have spoken

Charborough Park, with its tower and deer, 'the seat of Miss Sawbridge Erle Drax'

once in Parliament, to ask for a window to be opened, and to have addressed an election meeting thus: 'I am told that I have recently been slandered by certain people who say that I wish you to vote accordingly to your conscience. This is totally untrue. I wish you to vote for me.'

His funds provided the turnpike road from Wimborne to Puddletown with a wall of over two million bricks and three huge gates where it passes his park. These works were completed in 1842. On the other side of Charborough and Morden, wild boar were kept in Morden Park, until he shot them on deciding they were a vicious nuisance after a park-keeper and a horse had been savaged. Sawbridge was becoming an eccentric squire and would be remembered as the 'black sheep' of the family with that epithet having to compete with 'the old scoundrel'.

There were two daughters. After the death of his wife in 1853 – angry at the lack of a son and heir – Drax is said to have kept them imprisoned in Charborough, to prevent them finding husbands and thereby thwart the succession. Sawbridge's first daughter, Maria Caroline Erle Drax, died in 1885 and was buried in the family vault which runs the length of Charborough Chapel. She had been persuaded to will the estate for life first to her father and then the entail to her younger sister. The latter was Sarah Charlotte-Elizabeth Sawbridge Erle-Drax who managed to escape over the park wall and eloped with Colonel Francis Augustus Plunkett-Burton of the Coldstream Guards.

By pre-deceasing her father, in clause 27 of her will Maria left him 'all my real and personal estate not herein appointed'. He set about looting Charborough, borrowed £38,000 from the trustees of his marriage settlement, and embellished an estate at Holnest, near Sherborne, turning it into Holnest Park. Here he kept buffalo and trained dogs to hunt for truffles. His second home was Olantigh Towers, Kent, where he had an equestrian statue erected of himself – life-size, in a long cloak and raising his hat – erected beside the front-door. Greater eccentricities followed in Holnest churchyard, with the building of a large mock-Byzantine mausoleum. Drax rehearsed his own funeral, directing the cortège and swearing whenever the coffin and its dummy were jolted. The mausoleum had been provided with a letter-box. He arranged for *The Times* to be delivered daily after his death. That date (5 January 1887) was all that remained to be added to the marble memorial tablet. The mausoleum was demolished in 1935.

Sarah's one and only daughter, born in 1855, maintained tradition as the tenuous female link in the Charborough succession. Ernle Elizabeth Louisa Maria Grosvenor Burton married the Honourable John William Plunkett, second son of Admiral, Lord Dunsany (17th Baron in the Irish peerage) in 1877. Their only child, Admiral the Honourable Sir Reginald Aylmer Ranfurly Plunkett-Ernle-Erle-Drax (1880–1967) inherited the Morden estates from his mother in 1916, and assumed the additional names Ernle-Erle-Drax by royal licence. He set about buying back what he could of the family's dispersed possessions though he declined an opportunity to bid for a huge portrait of Sawbridge Drax and the Charborough Hounds.

Admiral Drax served in the Grand Fleet from 1914 and was present, on HMS *Lion*, as staff officer to Admiral Sir David Beatty, commanding battle cruisers in the Heligoland Action, Dogger Bank and Battle of Jutland. Having been awarded the Russian Order of St Stanislas, second class, in 1916, he won the Distinguished Service Order in 1918, when captain of HMS *Blanche*.
His post-war ascendancy was through the corridors of naval administration, from Director of the Royal Naval Staff College at Greenwich to President of the Naval Allied Control Commission in Berlin, and back home as aide-de-camp to

King George V. Director of Manning at the Admiralty was followed by a return to sea, as Commander-in-Chief America and West Indies Station, in 1932. He came back as Commander-in-Chief Plymouth and was then Commander-in-Chief The Nore on the outbreak of the Second World War. Having served as Naval ADC to King George VI he saw out the second half of the conflict as Commodore of Ocean Convoys.

Post-war retirement saw a succession of publications ranging from contemporary history to a pioneering study, in 1962, on Solar Heated Swimming Pools. As early as 1956 he was arguing that hereditary titles were a thing of the past, writing that a peerage, as 'a high honour often given by the Sovereign for signal service to the State' is devalued when handed on 'to a son or grandson who has done nothing whatever to earn it'. Henceforth every new peerage should be a life peerage.

Admiral Drax expanded the Morden estates to 13,000 acres with the purchase of Moorcourt estate, northwards from Westley Wood to the River Stour from Shapwick to Spetisbury, from George Onslow Churchill in 1920. To the east he bought fields at Henbury. The remainder of High Wood, covering 220 acres towards Lytchett Matravers, was also restored to the estate. Drifts of bulbs and other wildflowers have been preserved here and through the 712-acre Bere Wood towards Bere Regis. In 1926, one of the last direct links with the West Indies was gone, with the demise of the last of the Charborough herd of Brahmini or zebu cattle which were the main breed in Barbados. To help estate workers during the Depression he ran the Charborough Savings Bank from 1923 to 1931 'paying never less than 6 per cent interest'. Lady Kathleen Drax directed the modernisation of Charborough House and supervised its war service for British and American forces. Ancient houses were restored at Almer and Woolbridge Manor but vernacular architecture sustained numerous losses with many surplus cottages and barns being allowed to collapse and disappear into a well-wooded landscape that effectively forms Poole's western green belt.

The Admiral's son, Lieutenant Henry Walter Plunkett-Ernle-Erle-Drax RN (known as Walter Drax) married the Honourable Pamela Rose Weeks on 6 April 1957 and has consolidated his father's work. James Coldwell wrote a 75-page poem dedicated to Charborough, in 1950, of which a few lines will suffice:

> For many centuries Charborough has been given
> The prime of English craftsmen's skill and art;
> There is no other place so near to Heaven
> Which has so strong a claim to be England's heart.

CHETTLE HOUSE

Chafin — Castleman — Bourke

Dorset's finest Queen Anne style mansion, by Baroque architect Thomas Archer, is Chettle House. Archer was a pupil of Vanbrugh, who received the commission from George Chafin, and passed the work to his assistant. The resultant square brick lines are hidden by trees from an estate village where all 1060 acres of these rolling foothills of Cranborne Chase are owned by the Bourke family with the single exception of St Mary's parish church. The house was built for George Chafin, with five acres of formal landscaped grounds between the church and a grassy skyline bank. This dates back 3500 years and is a Neolithic long barrow.

Baroque architect Thomas Archer created Chettle House

More recent dates on the south wall of the house record its three dates of construction and restoration – '1710, 1846, 1912' – with the subsequent stage of its evolution having been low-key with a sympathetic modernisation that rescued it from wartime neglect. The furniture includes present-day masterpieces created on the estate by Rupert Brown whose personal transformation has been from competent carpenter into skilled craftsman.

Chettle's most colourful character was Rev. William Chafin who fell out with powerful neighbour Bubb Dodington of Eastbury House over the ancient game rights of Cranborne Chase. Having caught Dodington's keeper in the process of beating for game, Chafin proceeded to shoot dead the offending dogs, and challenge the man's master to meet him for a duel. Dodington rose to the occasion with diplomacy and charisma and the pair ended the day together having dinner at Eastbury. William Chafin enjoyed country sports for the remainder of his active life, until 'being struck by lightning at the age of eighty-five', after which he devoted his remaining days to recording the history of the Chase which retained its medieval status until the Disafforestation Act of 1830.

Portraits in Chettle House include Bourke family ancestor Edward Castleman who was the Wimborne lawyer who brought the railway to Dorset in 1845, along such a twisting and turning inland route from the New Forest to Wareham that it was known as 'Castleman's Corkscrew'. The ancient wealth was brought to the brink by death duties following the demise of a great uncle of present owner Patrick Bourke, who was born in 1937 and was evacuated to Chettle House on the outbreak of war in September 1939. Eventual ownership came with a legacy burdened with debts. 'We were an impoverished estate and it has taken decades to recover,' Patrick said in 1995. 'In fact it still holds us back to the present day and it has led to our creating little businesses as separate units so that each has its own accountancy, and you immediately know which is not paying or pulling its weight.'

Having confided that 'the place cannot afford a gardener' he went on to tell the author that it was as 'the worst dressed man in Dorset' that he received Princess Margaret on a surprise visit to the house in 1989. Patrick and Janet Bourke have recreated the gardens as a renowned example of what can be grown on chalk soil. They have balked at the usual practice of importing peat and other benign soil and instead work with what will tolerate their ground including many local and national rarities. These international imports often post-date the architecture which leads to some garden purists complaining that the plants are alien to the period.

Such a theme park or museum-like approach is shunned by the Bourkes. 'We answer that the only reason they were not planted in the beginning was because they were not available,' Janet replies. 'They would have used them if they had been.'

Another branch of the family, namely Edward and Barbara Bourke, opened the Castleman Hotel and Restaurant in a Victorian house in Chettle village which incorporates the walls of a medieval hunting lodge.

Patrick and Janet Bourke have re-created a setting worthy of Dorset's finest Queen Anne style house

***

CHIDEOCK MANOR

Arundell — Weld

Chideock Manor is one of the homes of the Arundell family whose nearby Chideock Castle was blown up in 1645 by order of the House of Commons for holding out for the Royalist cause. In 1802, Lord Arundell sold his Chideock estate to his cousin, Thomas Weld, of Lulworth Castle.

Humphrey Weld, the brother of Joseph Weld, told Mary Frampton that he had seen the certificate of Mrs Fitzherbert's wedding to King George IV, when he was Prince of Wales, and talked openly about it after the King's death in 1830. In recent times the manor has been the home of Lieutenant-Colonel Humphrey Weld, and his wife Frances, whose son Charles Weld rented the house to Prince Andrew, Duke of York, when he was flying helicopters from Portland.

***

Chideock Castle, the former western seat of the Arundel family, was left in ruins at the end of the Civil War

CHILDHAY MANOR

de Childhay — de Crewkerne — Bragge — Frost

Childhay, on the Temple Brook between Broadwindsor and Blackdown, now gives its name to the locally-made brand of farmhouse ice-cream. Built around a medieval hall, it also lends the name of its founding family to the nearby Somerset town, as it was the seat of the de Crewkerne family who absorbed the de Childhay line in the reign of Edward III. For the next three centuries the Crewkernes of Childhay held sway across much of the far west of Dorset and southern extremity of Somerset before the house passed to the Bragges of Sadborow and Thorncombe and became one of the bigger dairies of Dorset's western vale.

The ice-cream maker of modern times, Tim Frost, keeps his own herds of cows and goats and has made Childhay Manor the best known dairy farm in Dorset.

CLIFTON MAYBANK

Horsey — Phelips — Daniell

John Horsey (died 1531) of Clifton Maybank

The great mansion of the Horsey family at Clifton Maybank is largely no more, but its Tudor frontage and Jacobean gatehouse survive elsewhere, having been moved to Montacute and Hinton St George, Somerset by 1800. Its notable occupant was John Horsey (died 1531), an Esquire of the Body to King Henry VIII, who married Elizabeth Turges of Melcombe Bingham. Their son, Sir John Horsey (died 1546) purchased Sherborne Abbey and manor at the Dissolution of the Monasteries and the Abbey church for the townspeople. Son and heir Sir John Horsey (died 1564) married Edith Phelips of Montacute and owned some 18,000 acres of Somerset and Dorset.

The house's memorable visitor was Sir Thomas Wyatt (1503–42) who loved Anne Boleyn and invented the format for the sonnet. He died at Clifton Maybank after being taken there when stricken by fever while travelling through Sherborne.

The Horsey centuries, in both counties, ended with bankruptcy and the demise in a debtors' prison of Sir George Horsey (died 1644). The Phelips family looted the architecture during the following century. As for Clifton Maybank, its revival was inspired by Mr and Mrs Francis Daniell in Edwardian times, with a particular eye for colour co-ordinated settings contrasting greyish-green evergreen oaks against golden walls.

COMPTON HOUSE

Hawy — Stradling — Abington — Goodden

The golden walls of Compton House at Over Compton, modelled on Elizabethan Montacute and using the same Ham Hill quarries, are not as old as they look. The original house was badly damaged by fire in 1827 and the replacement dates from the 1840s. To confuse historians, there is a Tudor heraldic finial of a seated lion holding a shield, with the initials of John Horsey. Just four families have held Over Compton over the last millennium and they do not include the Horseys. The rogue pinnacle came from Clifton Maybank in the next valley.

Compton House was formerly known as Compton Hawy. The Hawy family were lords of the manor from the time of the Domesday Book, until the estate passed by marriage to the Stradling family from Glamorgan, in the late-thirteenth century. In 1542, Thomas Stradling sold it to Bristol merchant Thomas Abington for 700 marks. The Abingtons were at Compton Hawy for seven generations until George Abington approached his final illness in 1738. He sold Compton House to Robert Goodden of Martock in Somerset. This Robert Goodden, Sheriff of Dorset in 1746, stands in life-size marble in the adjacent parish church and bears a striking resemblance to the present-day Robert Goodden. The story of the succession shows, however, that keeping Gooddens in residence has been a close-run thing.

Colonel John Bernhard Harbin Goodden (1876–1951) retired to what was still known as Compton Hawy. His military service included the Boer War,

The Ham-stone walls of Compton House are younger than they look

Robert Goodden meets life-size ancestor Robert Goodden in Over Compton parish church

Lieutenant-Colonel J.R.P. Goodden of Compton House commanded the Dorsetshire Yeomanry from 1890 to 1900

Gallipoli and the Egyptian Expeditionary Force in its advance on Jerusalem and Damascus, being wounded in action against Senussi at Agagia. He was a director of the *Western Gazette* and Stuckeys Bank, also in the West Country, seeing it through take-over by the Westminster Bank. In 1937 he was High Sheriff of Dorset.

The family moved to West Coker Manor when Compton House was requisitioned during the Second World War. It became design offices for the Westland Aircraft Company and was not released by the Air Ministry until 1948. Meanwhile, the park had been put under the plough, and 'Dig for Victory' had even taken its toll on the main lawn. The house was also somewhat dilapidated when it passed to Rev. John Goodden who had moved during the war from Kings Norton, Birmingham, to the vicarage at Wilmington, near Dartford.

He and his eldest son, John Goodden, converted Compton House into flats. Another son, Robert Goodden (born 1940), had shown an interest in butterflies since moving from Birmingham to Kent at the age of four. He reared silkworms on mulberry leaves when he was a chorister at Salisbury Cathedral School and forwarded their silk to Lullingstone Silk Farm in the winter of 1952 as a practical contribution to Queen Elizabeth's coronation robe.

Robert Goodden founded Worldwide Butterflies (since pupated into Worldlife) in 1960, with the original global name being at his father's suggestion, at a time when Robert operated from a Charmouth attic and was too young to be a director of his own company. Then, with his wife Rosemary Goodden, he started the British Butterfly Conservation Society (now the charity Butterfly Conservation). Early in the next decade both bodies were firmly established around classroom-type accommodation and a maze of cages in the grounds of Compton House. Peter Scott arrived to give them encouragement and the public opening followed in 1973. The subsequent creation of a mini-jungle, in 1976, attracted massive television and press coverage. 'We were an instant success,' Robert Goodden recalls. 'We had devised a butterfly tunnel and it was the first time that people could experience a living butterfly display, with tropical plants.'

The family bombshell came when John Goodden decided to sell Compton House on the open market. Robert Goodden decided that he had to keep it in the family but the matter went to the brink. He only secured the finance – for what he described as 'a gloomy, cold and rotten building' – three days before it was to have been auctioned. By 1978 it was presentable and opened and then in 1979 the next opportunity was seized with the acquisition of Lullingstone Silk Farm after the death of Lady Hart Dyke. Its silkworms and equipment were brought to Over Compton where mulberry bushes were hastily planted.

Their first royal commission was the order for wedding dress material for Lady Diana Spencer on her marriage to the Prince of Wales. 'Prince Charles was still a bachelor and we had reared thousands of cocoons on leaves from mulberry trees from country house gardens all over Dorset and Somerset. It was a piece of really good fortune that we could provide the silk for the royal wedding dress, just in time. Vera Pitman of Nether Compton did the reeling for two different deniers of silk, which was very skilled work, for a month. Record attendances and publicity followed – 1981 was a very successful year with the royal wedding – and it is very sad that it ended the way it did.'

Announcing the transformation of Worldwide Butterflies into Worldlife, Robert Goodden mentioned the support it was giving to the Italian Ornithological Society to try and reduce the annual slaughter of 1500 birds of prey as they attempt to take their historic migratory route from the mainland to Sicily. 'They still have a wealth of natural history but so did we until we did so much to reduce it to at-risk levels. We've now learnt from our errors but it would be catastrophic, for our wildlife as well, if the southern Europeans repeat our mistakes. Hopefully I'll have as long to devote to this as I've had with Worldwide Butterflies. The important thing is to establish a secure base so that the work can continue beyond that, helping improve the world for people well into the twenty-first century.'

Butterfly man Robert Goodden has created Worldlife at Compton House

CRANBORNE MANOR

Cecil — Salisbury — Gascoyne-Cecil

Described by the Royal Commission on Historical Monuments as 'historically one of the most important domestic buildings in England', Cranborne Manor House incorporates the main walls of a fortified hunting lodge, built by King John in 1208. Its two-storey hall is vintage thirteenth century and the house is further acclaimed as 'one of the oldest surviving domestic buildings in the country, preserving its original forms to an extraordinary extent'.

Between them, William Cecil and son Robert held the highest office of State for fifty-four years, and masterminded the peaceful transition from Tudor to Stuart England. The reward was that Cranborne Manor was given to Robert Cecil, 1st Earl of Salisbury (1563–1612) by King James I who came there to hunt in Cranborne Chase. Civil War damage was repaired and the west wing rebuilt, in 1647, by architect Captain Richard Rider who had connections with Inigo Jones.

Cranborne Manor, architecturally and historically, is the most important house in Dorset

Rex Whistler's painting of the back view at Cranborne Manor

Mosaic portrait at Hatfield House of Robert Cecil, 1st Earl of Salisbury (1565–1612)

William Cecil, 2nd Earl of Salisbury (1591–1668)

Cranborne is the traditional seat of Viscount Cranborne, the son and heir of the Marquess of Salisbury, though these days the home of father and son can be interchangeable. Cranborne became the West Country second home of one of the most powerful political families in the land whose fortunes at their Jacobean seat of Hatfield, Hertfordshire, began by being synonymous with the interests of the first Queen Elizabeth and continue to the present day at Cranborne, through the new Elizabethan age, with weekend visits by the late Queen Mother in 1958 and 1972. Family historian Lord David Cecil regarded the house as their 'most exquisite architectural bequest to posterity' and described it as being 'as delicate an expression of the lyrical and romantic strains in the Elizabethan imagination as *A Midsummer Night's Dream* itself'. The thirteenth-century Dining Room is overlooked by a Minstrel's Gallery. Centuries of the best gossip in England have been heard here first.

Politics and the family effectively parted company for two hundred and fifty years before coming together again with a vengeance in the person of Robert Arthur Talbot Gascoyne-Cecil, 3rd Marquess of Salisbury (1830–1903), who also restored Cranborne Manor and the parish church. Bullied at Eton and naturally shy, he overcame his natural reserve to deliver stinging retorts in the House of Commons. Having been accused of acting more like an attorney than a statesman, Gladstone, as Chancellor of the Exchequer, demanded an apology the following day. Robert Cecil agreed demurely and added that he now realised that he had done a great injustice to attorneys.

In 1866 Disraeli persuaded the Prime Minister, Lord Derby, to appoint Cecil as Secretary for India but he resigned the following year on an issue of principle, having disagreed over a bill to widen popular voting rights. Not for the first time, instead of resenting being regarded as shifty and devious, Disraeli regarded the resignation as being to Robert Cecil's credit and referred to him as the most honest and intelligent person in the Conservative Party.

Meanwhile, in 1868 Robert succeeded his father, becoming the 3rd Marquess of Salisbury. Disraeli reinstated him as Secretary of State for India and from now on Salisbury's career never looked back. Though reluctant, he was sent to an international conference in Constantinople as the Turkish Empire imploded, complaining that it would involve 'sea-sickness, much French, and failure'. All three proved true but Disraeli regarded his diplomatic despatches as brilliant and promoted him to Foreign Secretary in 1878.

Russia won the war over control of the Turkish colonies and changed the balance of power in eastern Europe. Salisbury's moral scruples were now compromised by pragmatism and he lied in Parliament about secret negotiations with the Russians. Having categorically denied these were taking place he later announced their success with an amended treaty, ceding Cyprus to Britain and safeguarding sea-routes in the Mediterranean, and returned to cheering crowds in London.

Later, in full power as the leader of his party and the nation, he coupled the positions of Prime Minister and Foreign Secretary in three administrations, covering most of the years between 1885 and 1902 when Britain was still unchallenged as the most powerful nation on earth, though Germany, Japan, Russia and the United States were all gaining strength. His imperialist imperative was applied with cautious conciliation and consolidated colonial interests in Burma, Sudan, Zanzibar and South Africa (at the price of the Boer War). He refused to take advantage of troubles in China and Turkey, controversially in the latter case, as it involved ignoring the Armenian massacres of 1897. Resignation was at his choice and timing, on concluding the Boer War, in favour of his nephew, A.J. Balfour. Robert Cecil had expanded the British

Empire, to its zenith, by 600 million square miles and 100 million inhabitants. Queen Victoria regarded him as her greatest (and last) Prime Minister.

His eldest son and heir, James Edward Hubert Gascoyne-Cecil, 4th Marquess of Salisbury (1861–1947), was Lord Privy Seal and Leader of the House of Lords between 1925 and 1929. He opposed Home Rule in India and adopted other lost causes. In the English countryside he was the essence of a feudal but paternalistic landlord, delighting in regular visitations to both the Hatfield and Cranborne estates, where he called on every tenant and often modernised cottages at his expense. He spoke of Dorset as 'a breath of fresh air'. Some of the replacement artisan housing in and around Cranborne was to his own design. Once, at Hatfield, Gerald Balfour told a man he was a Philistine. 'What is a Philistine?' he asked. Lord Salisbury answered from afar; 'A Philistine is a man who is killed by the jawbone of an ass.'

Two of Robert Cecil's other sons also had distinguished political careers though in conflicting directions. Third son Robert, full name Edgar Algernon Robert, 1st Viscount Cecil (1864–1958) had enough of war as a Minister of Blockade against Germany and negotiated disarmament treaties in the 1920s, winning the Nobel peace prize in 1937. Fifth son, Lord Hugh Richard Heathcote Cecil (1869–1956), joined Winston Churchill in heading the independent group in the House of Commons.

Robert Arthur James 'Bobbety' Cecil, 5th Marquess of Salisbury (1893–1972), a Grenadier in the Great War, was MP for South Dorset from 1929 to 1940. In 1941 he entered the Lords as Baron Cecil of Essendon and was Secretary of State for the Dominions, Lord Privy Seal and Leader of the House of Lords, from 1942 to 1945 and again from 1951 to 1957. He was Secretary for Commonwealth Relations in 1952. All that sounds impressive but he might have climbed much further. After dinner on 20 April 1944, Winston Churchill confided to John Colville that he had twice considered the possibility of promoting Bobbety to replace Anthony Eden as Foreign Secretary 'but when he wasn't ill he would be obstinate'. Churchill joked that these were consecutive weaknesses: 'It would be a question of a fortnight's illness alternating with a fortnight's obstinacy.'

As he aged, he collected lost causes and took up instances of injustice, and was usually just a resignation letter away from following his conscience. Three such departures took place and the last saw events turning full-circle. Lord Salisbury resigned as Lord President of the Council in 1957 when the Government released Archbishop Makarios who championed the cause of

Lady Catherine Howard, 2nd Countess of Salisbury, in 1673

James Cecil, 7th Earl and 1st Marquess of Salisbury (1748–1823), painted by George Romney

(Left) James Cecil, 4th Earl of Salisbury (1666–94) with his eldest sister, Lady Catherine Cecil (1663–88)

(Right) James Cecil, 5th Earl of Salisbury (1691– 1728)

Robert Cecil, 3rd Marquess of Salisbury, drawn by George Richmond in 1861

James Cecil, 4th Marquess of Salisbury (1861–1947) as Viscount Cranborne, in the Hertfordshire Yeomanry in 1882

The 4th Marchioness of Salisbury, Lady Cicely Alice Gore (1867–1955) with youngest child Lord David Cecil

independence for Cyprus which Salisbury's grandfather had brought into the British Empire.

Bobbety married Betty, the daughter of Lord Richard and Lady Moyra Cavendish, and was a close friend of King George VI and Queen Elizabeth, the late Queen Mother. Regarded as the epitome of true-blue aristocracy, he was succeeded by his son Robert Edward Peter Cecil, 6th Marquess of Salisbury (born 1916), who was MP for Bournemouth West in the early 1950s and President of the right-wing Monday Club.

His son, Robert Michael James Cecil, Viscount Cranborne (born 1946), sometime Member of Parliament for South Dorset, epitomises the family weakness – or strength – of principle ahead of ambition. 'An episode of my irresponsible youth,' is how he described the controversial proposing of Rhodesian Foreign Minister P.K. Van Der Byl for membership of the Turf Club, at a time when the latter had labelled blacks as 'savages'. Ireland then put a stop to Robert Cranborne's first step up the Governmental ladder, as Parliamentary Private Secretary to Foreign Office Minister Cranley Onslow. Just six days later he had to resign, on finding it impossible to vote for an Irish measure, and reflected that acceptance of the post was an error; 'I should never have accepted it, given my views on Ireland, but Cranley was a mate and I thought I could grit my teeth and vote in favour. In the event I couldn't.'

Arriving back in Britain in April 1992 with Oxford historian and polemicist Professor Norman Stone, fresh from dinner with the chief minister in Slovakia, Robert Cranborne received a call from John Major. 'I've been trying to contact you for days,' the Prime Minister said, as he proceeded to offer Viscount Cranborne the position of Parliamentary Under-Secretary of State for Defence. 'I believe the demotic term for how I felt is gobsmacked,' said Robert, who proceeded to consult with his father and then accepted the job.

In order to take it, to sit for the Government in the House of Lords, he went through an unusual procedure of renouncing his courtesy title of Viscount Cranborne, as heir to the Marquess of Salisbury, in exchange for a life peerage. Finally, after Tony Blair's election victory in 1997, he was Opposition Leader of the Conservatives in the Lords until the end of the millennium when he again followed family tradition by speaking without counting the cost, which in his case was instant dismissal by Party leader William Hague. Yet another Robert Cecil, or Robert Cranborne as he is known, was in his wilderness years.

He married Hannah Stirling, the daughter of Highland landowner Bill Stirling, in 1970 and they have five children. The couple's significance towards the end of the twentieth century was in acting as the host and hostess of the 'Blue Chip' grouping from the 1979 Parliamentary intake of Conservative MPs who found themselves with rooms along the same staircase. The five were Tristan Garel-Jones, Christopher Patten, John Patten, Richard Needham and William Waldegrave. These five powerful insiders are credited with plotting the coup of November 1990 that drove Mrs Thatcher from office. Robert Cecil would be delighted that Robert Cranborne was still running the nation from within his ancient walls.

Universal telephones have ended a more recent institution. When the Marquess came down by train from Waterloo to visit the Viscount at Cranborne he would telegram 'CRANBORNE CRANBORNE' from the nearest mail-line station with the message 'SALISBURY SALISBURY'. Vice versa, with son coming down to father, the message would be 'SALISBURY CRANBORNE' from 'CRANBORNE SALISBURY'.

CREECH GRANGE

Lawrence — Bond — Hayward

The Tudor mansion in the northern shadow of the Purbeck Hills was built by Sir Oliver Lawrence (died 1559) on former Bindon Abbey lands in about 1545. Brother-in-law of Sir Thomas Wriothesley, Henry VIII's Lord Chancellor, he bought it from Sir John Horsey of Clifton Maybank who acquired it at the Dissolution of the Monasteries. Sir Oliver Lawrence became Collector of Customs for the Port of Poole.

The Lawrence shields-of-arms are in the parish church at Steeple, on the other side of the hills, carved in stone and on panels in the barrel-vaulted roof. The heraldic 'stars and stripes' – correctly termed 'bars and mullets' – of the Washington family are quartered by the crusader cross of the Lawrence family with the initials 'D.L.E.' for Edward Lawrence and the date 1616. Thus the Creech Grange family is linked with a famous descendant, namely the first

Creech Grange and its private chapel (top left) in 1857

American President, George Washington (1732–99). The family connection dates from the marriage of Edmund Lawrence and Agnes de Wessington in 1390.

The other lasting name arrived in 1691 and the Bonds remained in residence at Creech Grange for four centuries. Robert Bond of Hatch Beauchamp, Somerset, acquired Lutton Farm, Steeple, by marriage in the reign of Henry VI. Their notable descendant was Sir Thomas Bond who gave his name to Bond Street in London, which became coupled with New Bond Street in the capital and the ironically-named Old Bond Street around the corner from Creech Grange.

The families of Bond and Lawrence had their critical liaison when widower Denis Bond (died 1658), the Cromwellian member of Parliament for Dorchester and then for Weymouth, chose Lucy Lawrence as his second wife and lived with her at Lutton from 1622. Bond's death, on 30 August 1658, coincided with 'the windiest day that had before happened for twenty years' and became the butt of a Royalist joke when Oliver Cromwell followed him on 3 September 1658. Puns were in vogue and the saying was that 'the Devil made sure he took his Bond for Oliver's appearance'.

The younger son of Denis and Lucy, Sir Nathaniel Bond (1634–1707) was MP for Corfe Castle and then Dorchester, and Recorder of Weymouth, being knighted on appointment as King's Serjeant in 1693. He used his status and wealth to buy the estate at Lutton from his elder brothers, John and William, and acquired the reversion of the lands over the Purbeck Hills at Creech in 1686, from John Lawrence. Creech Grange fell into the possession of Nathaniel Bond in 1691. His second marriage was to Lewis Williams of Shitterton, Bere Regis, and their sons were Denis and John.

Denis Bond (1706–46) appreciated the scenic potential of the setting around Creech Grange, in a triangle between what was then windswept downland, virgin heathland, and the wild conical shaped eminence of Creech Barrow Hill.

The south side of Creech Grange moments before a summer storm

His lasting landmark on the Purbeck skyline is a Gothic eye-catcher called Grange Arch on the map but known locally as Bond's Folly. This had a double meaning as his other folly was a major corruption scandal in the 1720s as a result of which he was expelled from the House of Commons, where he sat as the member for Poole, for 'fraudulently and clandestinely' contracting to sell state-owned lands in the Lake District for much less than they were worth.

Denis Bond also created the grounds and commissioned Blandford architect Francis Cartwright on a £1300 scheme for 'building about the house'. He extended the southern facade in Palladian style and built a chapel in the grounds, from the ruins of Holme Priory, shortly before his death. The eastern frontage of the main house was rebuilt entirely a century later, by Nathaniel Bond in 1846, but despite the scale of the changes in appearance it closely matches the Tudor original.

Nathaniel Bond married Lady Selina Jane Scott, daughter of the 2nd Earl of Eldon from Encombe House, and their barrister son, John Wentworth Garneys Bond (1865–1948), was Clerk of the House of Commons from 1890 till 1926.

In 1981, after the death of Lieutenant-Colonel Ashley Bond, Creech Grange became the home of Parkstone-born businessman Norman Hayward. Under his directorship Yeovil Town became the most successful football club in the West Country. His wife, Pat who died in 1992, established the first cancer charity shop in Britain, at Wareham, and established a chain which now crosses the country.

The man and his mansion, with Norman Hayward and the east front, at Creech Grange

CRICHEL HOUSE

Napier — Sturt — Alington — Marten

The arms of the Napier and Sturt families, united at Crichell

With the removal of the competition, after demolition of most of Eastbury House, that at Crichel was left as Dorset's greatest eighteenth-century seat, thanks to two visionary owners separated by a timely fire.

The first was third son of judge Sir Gerard Napier and Margaret Colles. The dilettante Sir Nathaniel Napier (1636–1709) married Blanche Wyndham, the daughter of Sir Hugh Wyndham, and moved from Crichel to Edmondsham House. From there he organised the renovation of the main family homes of Middlemarsh House and Crichel House, while representing the county and various Dorset boroughs in Parliament, on and off from 1677 until 1705. A linguist and traveller, the 'ingenious gentleman' also dabbled in art and architecture, and was a competent painter and draughtsman.

Sir Nathaniel's only surviving son, also Sir Nathaniel Napier, sat for Dorchester in nine Parliaments between 1695 and 1722. In 1742, during the time of Sir William Napier, the fourth baronet, Crichel House was destroyed by fire. His family wealth enabled a swift start to rebuilding but the work dragged on for years.

When the sixth baronet died in 1765 the 18,000-acre estate passed to Humphry Sturt (1725–86), a cousin, and remained with his descendants into the new millennium.

Reflections of Crichel House and private chapel in 1857

Humphry Sturt turned to the rebuilding of Crichel House and brought big ideas. He stretched the 75 by 60 feet three-storey floor-plan to a length of 130

The south front of Crichel House in 1970

feet along the east side. He also overwhelmed the original provincial look the Bastard brothers from Blandford had created. Sturt's south front is perfectly proportioned, with a classical portico of pillars inset as a colonnade, which rises to 60 per cent of the general roof-line. Sideways it occupies 40 per cent of the available width. There is something about these proportions that cannot be accidental.

Their creator was Sturt himself. Not for him any fussy detail but rather the assertive precision of someone who knew just what he wanted. He was congratulated by the agricultural writer Arthur Young in 1771; 'Mr Sturt (who is his own architect) has contrived it so uncommonly well that the whole will unite to form a noble house.'

It does indeed. Some of the refinements, such as the neo-classical interior decorations, have been attributed to James Wyatt, the famous architect, who was travelling the highway to the north of the estate while working on Milton Abbey. That scheme may have been an effort to keep up with Sturt. Though he never demolished an entire town he had in 1771–72 moving his village and putting it in the next parish. The Moor Crichel cottagers were rehoused at New Town, a linear hamlet half a mile north-east of Witchampton.

In their place he put some water. The landscape vision required a lake – half-moon in shape and more serpentine than the later puddle-shape at Milton Abbas – which was achieved by damming the River Allen. From 1760 the new Crichel House filled with children. Humphry Ashley Sturt was the first of 16 offspring that Humphry Sturt and the former Mary Pitfield, from Hoxton, produced.

By 1762 Humphry Sturt was looking for further landscape challenges. With his cousin, Sir Gerard Napier, he bought Brownsea Island, in Poole Harbour, for £650. That fully stretched his talents. Out of obligation he served as a Member of Parliament for three decades, from 1754, but remained speechless. Politics to him was the status quo rather than a matter for thought and most of the time he saw no point in attending Parliament. Jeremy Bentham found Sturt uninteresting and Sturt found philosophical concepts intrinsically boring. When he found his continued candidature would be opposed he stood down with dignity, though he still felt he could have won an election if it had been forced. Two years later he died at Bath, when the spa waters failed to revive his declining health, and was succeeded by his younger son, Charles Sturt.

Henry Gerard Sturt, as new peer Baron Alington of Crichel, in 1876

The large classical lake-side temple briefly housed Princess Charlotte Augusta (1796–1817) when in 1814 she defied her father, George IV, and ended her engagement to Prince William of Orange. The unhappy princess was punished by the dismissal of every member of her household and was sent into rural exile. The princess found her true love in 1816 and married Prince Leopold of Saxe-Coburg. She died the following year, hours after the birth of their still-born son, to a great tide of national grief. With her death the royal succession moved to the Duke of Kent and young Princess Victoria who took the throne on the death of William IV in 1837.

Steward of the Jockey Club and MP for Dorchester, Henry Gerard Sturt, 1st Baron Alington (1825–1904), married Lady Augusta Bingham, daughter of the 3rd Earl of Lucan. Lord Alington owned Derby winner 'Common'. 'Brigantine', a yearling he sold for 150 guineas, won the Oaks and Ascot Gold Cup in 1869. His hobby was White Farm, a section of Racing Stud Farm at Crichel, where he collected white species of animals and birds, and albino specimens of non-white types, from all over the globe. The Sultan of Constantinople presented him with a white mule. Fanny, a white hind, followed her keeper around like a dog.

The heir to the 18,000-acre estate, Humphrey Napier Sturt, 2nd Baron Alington (1859–1919), married Lady Feodorowna Yorke, daughter of the 5th Earl of Hardwicke. Their elder son, Captain the Honourable Gerard Sturt (1893–1918), joined the Coldstream Guards and was wounded in the Battle of Marne in 1914. He died on the very day that the Great War ended when the Armistice was declared. His brother Napier George Henry Sturt, 3rd Baron Alington (1896–1940), married Lady Mary Sibell Ashley-Cooper, eldest daughter of the 9th Earl of Shaftesbury. He died of pneumonia while serving as a liaison officer in Egypt. The only child was a daughter and the title became extinct on the death of the 3rd Lord Alington.

The Crichel shoot, traditionally one of Dorset's biggest, in 1900

King Edward VII visiting the Alington family at Crichel

The 2nd Lord and Lady Alington (standing beside FX 2) and assembled automobiles of the country house set at Crichel House in 1905

Mary Anna Sturt inherited her father's Crichel estate. In 1949 she married Lieutenant-Commander George Gosslin 'Toby' Marten (1918–97). He had been 'hammering hell' out of German fortifications in the Adriatic from the destroyer HMS *Wilton* in 1944 and was a post-war equerry to King George VI. The couple were soon battling the Government over de-requisition of Crichel Down Bombing Range. Instead of offering it back to the estate, the Air Ministry passed it to the Ministry of Agriculture and Fisheries which handed it to the Commissioners of Crown Lands, who found a tenant. The outcome was the 'Crichel Down scandal' of proven bureaucratic maladministration. It resulted in the resignation of Conservative Agriculture Minister Sir Thomas Dugdale, in 1954, and the return of Crichel Down to Mrs Marten.

Toby Marten went on to win back Tarrant Rushton Aerodrome from Flight Refuelling and revived the Crichel tradition of racehorse breeding with the filly 'Dead Certain'. He was High Sheriff of Dorset in 1961. For years his name remained on the approved list of prospective candidates issued by Conservative Central Office but no constituency ever selected him. The party never forgave him for putting Sir Thomas Dugdale in the political graveyard.

DEWLISH HOUSE

Baskett — Skinner — Michel — de Montmorency — Dilllon — Boyden

T he Develish Brook, an intermittent chalk stream, gives its name to Dewlish House on the south side of Dewlish village, towards the woods on Park Hill. Though rebuilt in Queen Anne style it is on a much older site and has the walls and mosaics of a Roman villa in its grounds. The property was in the hands of the Baskett family, until 1663 when Thomas Baskett sold it to London merchant Nicholas Skinner. His son, Thomas Skinner, built the present house in 1702 but it was sold some time after the death of his son, the second Thomas Skinner (died 1756).

The purchaser was David Robert Michel of Kingston Russell. His son was General John Michel and grandson Field Marshal Sir John Michel (1804–86). The latter served in the Kaffir Wars of 1846–47 and 1851–53. From 1858 he was on the Bombay staff in the run-up to the Indian Mutiny. He marched 1700 miles with his Mhow Division to capture a notable rebel, Tantia Topee, who was immediately subjected to court-martial and hanged on a charge of being in arms against the British. The legality of that sentence was disputed but Michel's later imperial adventure was remembered far longer.

On 12 October 1860, he led the 1st Division into Peking, as an army of occupation, and six days later burnt the Yuen-ming-yuen, the Emperor's summer palace to the ground. It was retaliation for the Chinese treatment of British captives. The impetuous Field-Marshal died at Dewlish House and is buried in the north aisle of the parish church.

Dewlish House in 1857

His daughter married into the Montmorency family and her husband continued the military tradition. The son of Viscount Mountmorres, Lieutenant the Honourable Raymond Hervey de Montmorency (1867–1900) charged with the 21st Lancers at Omdurman, Sudan, to win the Victorian Cross in 1898. Two years later he was killed by the Boers at the other end of Africa.

His widow, Lady Frankfort de Montmorency, lived at Dewlish House until her death in 1936. She was succeeded by the Honourable Rachel de Montmorency and the house was occupied by Colonel Eric FitzGerald Dillon, 19th Viscount Dillon (1881–1946) who had married a grand-daughter of Sir John Michel. He served with distinction in the Boer War, Great War and Second World War, and the title passed to his only son, Major Michael Eric Dillon, 20th Viscount Dillon (1911–79).

In recent times Dewlish House has been the home of Caroline and James Boyden whose family also own Chebbard Farm on the other side of the village. There is also an old Manor House at Dewlish, rebuilt in 1866, which is now Manor Farm.

DUNTISH COURT

Foy — Holford — Douglass

Sir William Chambers, the architect of Somerset House, built Castle Hill in the foothills rising from the western side of the Blackmore Vale at Buckland Newton, and went on to rebuild Milton Abbey. Castle Hill, later known as Duntish Court, was built in 1760 for Fitzwalter Foy (died 1781) and his wife Elizabeth Maria (died 1806). A Palladian mansion, with corridors extending to flanking pavilions, it stood on land that had been sold by John Churchill, 1st Duke of Marlborough, to Foy's grandfather. Churchill had left his Dorset roots for the opulence of Blenheim Palace.

In Victorian and Edwardian times it was the residence of Thomas Holford and became derelict after the death of his widow. It was eventually demolished, in 1965, revealing the original delicate brickwork which had been clad in stone. The much smaller present-day Duntish Court is the home of Alexander and Susan Douglass.

EASTBURY HOUSE

Dodington — Bubb — Temple — Farquharson

Built to palatial proportions, and third in size nationally behind Blenheim Palace and Castle Howard, Eastbury House in the Tarrant valley was Dorset's largest country house. It was built to Sir John Vanbrugh's designs between 1717 and 1738 for George Dodington (died 1720) and his nephew George Bubb Dodington, 1st Baron Melcombe (1691–1762). It looks big enough today but the present Eastbury House is just one wing of a Baroque extravaganza. There were five courts stretching 570 feet. By the time of its completion, by Roger Morris, Vanbrugh had been dead for twelve years and was out of fashion. Palladian style had arrived.

George Bubb Dodington built Eastbury House to palatial proportions

The arms of Farquharson of Langton House and Eastbury

Eastbury cost more than £140,000 which was astronomical in those days and equals tens of millions in present values. George Bubb, the son of a Weymouth pharmacist, brought to completion his uncle's ambition and vision. Dodington had been a Lord of Admiralty and the natural habitat of George Bubb Dodington, as he styled himself, was also in the corridors of power. He had six Parliamentary seats in his pocket – Weymouth and Melcombe Regis (four members), Winchelsea and Bridgwater – and had been Envoy Extraordinary to Spain. Lord of the Treasury followed as he made political alliances and projected himself as a Maecenas.

Something of a poet, he dedicated verses to Horace Walpole: 'In power a servant, out of power a friend.' His wit was highly regarded, as was his patronage, which went to many of the best writers of the age. Those chosen for sponsorship included Edward Young, James Thomson, Henry Fielding, Richard Bentley and Paul Whitehead. Showing 'all the courtly and profound devotion of a Spaniard, with the ease and gaiety of a Frenchman towards the men', Bubb Dodington clothed 'his bulk and corpulency' from 'a wardrobe loaded with rich and flaring suits'. He gave 'the picture of an ancient courtier in his gala habit or Quin in his stage dress'.

Bubb Dodington had a national reputation for high living, as did his steward, William Doggett, at Eastbury. As Dodington was incessantly absent, Doggett did little to cover his frauds, and a legend was handed on for generations in the former Bugle Horn Inn. News reached the house that the London mail coach had stopped on the Blandford road, and that the successor squire, Lord Temple, had stepped down from it. His arrival was totally unexpected and Doggett had the evidence of fiddles strewn around the house with only minutes in which to conceal things. He therefore did the only decent thing of his life and shot himself.

Folklore says he haunts the stone-flanked park gates and comes with a legend that makes him the most sinister of Dorset ghosts. Being unworthy of burial in consecrated land, he is said to emerge at night from his tomb at Tarrant Gunville, as a vampire, to drink the blood of sleeping villagers. The tale was given a new lease of life in 1845 when bodies were disturbed during the restoration of St Mary's Church. That of William Doggett had not decomposed; the legs were bound with a ribbon of yellow silk.

The outer entrance to Eastbury, from Tarrant Gunville, in 1857

Dodington was created 1st Baron Melcombe of Melcombe Regis in 1761 and died the following year. He had no children and Eastbury passed to Lord Temple, who gave up trying to find a paying tenant, and became so desperate that he offered £200 a year to anyone who would live in it! No one would. The house began to decay and Temple was created 1st Marquis of Buckingham in 1784. He ordered demolition, of all but one wing, in 1795.

A collection of mounds, towards the prehistoric Chettle long barrow, are the survivors of 14 tree-covered hillocks that were part of the original landscaping of the original Eastbury Park. Grand formal gardens, including a canal and temple, were abandoned in 1782. Residual parkland still covers 100 acres.

The first photographer, Thomas Wedgwood (1771–1805), died at Eastbury House and is buried in the parish church at Tarrant Gunville which has a marble tablet to record that he was the son of the famous potter Josiah Wedgwood. In 1802 he had made a 'shadow graph' of a fern leaf which had been placed in strong sunlight on to a sheet of paper coated with salt of silver. He knew nothing of the qualities of hyposulphite which could have made his pictures permanent.

His circle of friends included Samuel Taylor Coleridge, William Wordsworth, Sir John Leslie, Sydney Smith, Thomas Campbell, Sir Humphry Davy and Thomas Poole. Thomas Wedgwood's elder sister made her contribution to science by giving birth to Charles Darwin.

James John Farquharson (1785–1871) bought Eastbury House in 1806 and established kennels for 75 couple of fox-hounds and stables for some 50 horses. He became Dorset's premier huntsman, running the Eastbury estate in tandem with Langton House, downstream from Blandford in the Stour valley. He was succeeded by Henry Richard Farquharson MP and Henry Frank Ward Farquharson.

Hunting squire of Langton and Eastbury, James John Farquharson, painted by Sir Francis Grant in 1858

Inner entrance (left, with pine trees on top) and surviving wing of Eastbury House, in 1857

EDMONDSHAM HOUSE

Servington — Hussey — Monro

The Servington family were followed at Edmondsham House by the Husseys in the fifteenth century. Its 1589-dated Elizabethan mansion was built by Thomas Hussey. Their male line expired with the death of the third Thomas Hussey of Edmondsham in 1745.

Ownership of the house passed through the Fry and Bower families to a succession of Monros. Hector Monro and Hector Edmond Monro were followed by Lieutenant-Commander Hector Richard Monro. The first two Monros are commemorated by their initials on the village pump which they provided in 1884, with ironwork that looks like an outsized sewing machine. 'It still works,' a young boy told me in 1995, after the winter rain. 'You can have a go but it will take a lot of pumping to get it started.'

Edmondsham House in 1800

ENCOMBE HOUSE

Pitt — Scott — Eldon

The arms of Scott of Encombe, the Earls of Eldon

As near to perfection as any Dorset great house, Encombe's pleasantly simple south-facing frontage was completed in 1770, by John Pitt who had bought 'the much decayed' ancient seat of the Culliford family in 1734. Philanthropist William Morton Pitt (1754–1836), the son of Marcia and John Pitt of Encombe, was the second of the William Pitts of the late-eighteenth century. The first was an entirely different creature – the mastermind of the 'Pitt and Plunder' system of British Government, which created poverty and distress for Dorset cousin William to alleviate.

William Pitt of Encombe inherited a vast fortune from his father and dissipated it on good works. Sir Tresham Lever, in *The House of Pitt*, writes that because of his spending 'the wealthiest branch of the family sank into the obscurity of the landless middle class.' His personal programme of social works included a cordage manufactory at Kingston, a fish-curing plant at Swanage, and spinning and bleaching school at Fordington, Dorchester, and a hat-making works in the new County Gaol. The latter he had been instrumental in rebuilding in 1787 and was delighted that in the improved regime many prisoners 'are now behaving well and maintaining themselves and their families by their own industry.'

Though hardly a Parliamentarian by the standards of his illustrious family, he represented Poole from 1780 to 1790 and then sat as one of the county members for Dorset, through to 1826, describing it as a career which 'though not brilliant has been laborious for forty-five years.'

In the process he lost the great houses at Kingston Maurward, Stinsford, and Encombe House, as well as Kingston village, and put his final cash and energies into turning the Manor House, Swanage, into what became the Royal Victoria Hotel. In the process of this, he wrote at the age of seventy-one, 'both Mrs Pitt and I have beggared ourselves for some time past toward the accomplishment of this objective.'

Victorian print of Encombe after Scott family values and the politics of patronage turned it into the greatest of Purbeck seats

View from the south, of Encombe House and the Golden Bowl, from its lake in 1857

A totally different personality, former Newcastle coal-trader John Scott, 1st Earl of Eldon (1751–1838) became Lord High Chancellor of England in 1801 and held the position, virtually continuously, until 1827. He amassed a fortune as the nation's top attorney and bought the idyllic Encombe estate with its mansion in the Golden Bowl between Corfe Castle and the English Channel in 1807. He had been created Baron Eldon in 1799 and was created the Earl of Eldon in 1821. A supporter of William Pitt and the subject of ridicule from fellow Parliamentarian Richard Brinsley Sheridan, his favourite saying was that 'a lawyer should live like a hermit and work like a horse'. He progressed through the upper echelons of power to Solicitor General in 1788, Attorney General in 1793 and Chief Justice of Common Pleas in 1799.

His notable legal cases included the prosecution of Horne Tooke and depriving atheist poet Percy Bysshe Shelley of custody of his children, after the suicide of his wife, Harriet Shelley, in 1816. Shelley's negative religious beliefs were cited by Scott as the grounds for his decision. As a dominant member of the Cabinet he was resolute against the threat from Napoleon but rejected calls for Roman Catholic emancipation and opposed the growing clamour for reform of the voting system. He resisted the gathering momentum for extending the franchise and changing constituency boundaries.

Admirers thought him 'almost the ideal of manly beauty'. He was a prodigious port drinker and a lousy shot: 'With a gun he can kill nothing but time.' Critics linked his office with financial corruption. In the words of Cyrus Reading, one of his contemporaries; 'He had a sterile soul for all things earthly except money, doubts and the art of drawing briefs.'

John Scott, 3rd Earl of Eldon (1845–1926) of Encombe House

Eldon employed William Bushrod of Weymouth to refit the interior of the house, installing new moulded fireplaces, moulded ceiling and cornices, in a series of repairs between 1811 and 1813 that followed a fire. When he died, Eldon was worth £700,000. Coming from Love Lane, Newcastle, he had moved from industry to Government, becoming the last major recipient of the plunder system of British politics, which subsidised the lavish hospitalities of Encombe and his Hamilton Place town-house with £40,000 legally seized from bankruptcies, lunacies and wardships. 'If we, by our industry have acquired a degree of opulence and distinction which we could not reasonably have looked for, let us be thankful to that Government to whose favour we are, in a great measure, indebted for success,' Eldon said in the smoothness of self-justification. 'And do not let us by any rash attempt upon our constitution, put it out of the power of our children to rise to similar situations.'

This chance in life he presented to his own but Eldon kept some other children in their place. He had the will of a Mr Troutback, who left £100,000 for a charity school at Wapping, set aside and the money given to George IV to help liquidate the royal debts. The money bequeathed to clothe, educate and maintain poor children was applied to meet the furniture bills, tailoring, haberdashery and riotous living of the Prince Regent. Eldon took his time considering such matters – amounting to applied indecision – 'due to an extreme scrupulosity, which caused him to review the case long after he had in fact exhausted it.' He refused to apply injunctions to protect behaviour which he considered to be immoral, seditious or irreligious. His satirical epithet, in the *Sun* newspaper, was 'Dil-a-Tory'.

Eldon's two sons, John Scott (1774–1805) and William Henry Scott (1795–1832), both pre-deceased him, though John had married Henrietta Elizabeth Ridley, the daughter of Sir Matthew White Ridley. They produced a son, John Scott on 10 December 1805, and would thereby eventually enable the title to jump a generation.

The 40-feet high Encombe Obelisk, tapering in Egyptian needle-style, stands at the 425-feet contour above Quarry Wood at the landward end of the Golden Bowl. It was erected for Sir William Scott, 1st Baron Stowell (1745–1836), the Earl of Eldon's brother, who was a close friend of Dr Samuel Johnson and the pre-eminent draughtsman of international maritime law. Another monument, in the South Gwyle, is the Rock Bridge which is a primitive-style megalithic construction over a gully in the wooded ravine. It is built in rustic style with great semi-tooled boulders of Purbeck stone, without cement, and monolithic uprights to give a bizarre appearance. I am sure that it was built 'as a piece of fun' by architect George Stanley Repton, the youngest son of landscape gardener Humphry Repton, who eloped with Lady Elizabeth Scott in 1817. He made his peace with his father-in-law, the 1st Earl, in 1820 and henceforth the estate had the services of its own Gothic architect, until his death in 1858. Elizabeth's sister, Lady Frances Jane Scott, married the rector of Corfe Castle, Rev. Edward Bankes, in 1820.

The girls' nephew, John Scott, 2nd Earl of Eldon (1805–54) was their father's heir, being created Viscount Encombe in 1821 and inheriting the main title, on his grandfather's death in 1838. His son, John Scott, 3rd Earl of Eldon (1845–1926) played a pivotal part in local affairs and enriched the Isle of Purbeck with one of the best Victorian churches in the land, built to cathedral-like specifications by George Edmund Street at Kingston, between 1874 and 1880. Purbeck needed a railway more than another church, the *City Press* newspaper growled, and Eldon duly co-operated with its construction across his land, from 1883 to 1885. The Encombe estate then covered 25,800 acres and included substantial property around Stowell Park at Chedworth, Gloucestershire. John Scott, the 4th Earl of Eldon (1899–1976) was a Lord-in-Waiting to King George VI throughout his reign, from 1937 to 1952, and to Queen Elizabeth II until 1968. He saw the estates reduced to the still substantial 10,000 acres though the Scott family lands in the Isle of Purbeck would be reduced further, with heathland at Arne being sold to the Royal Society for the Protection of Birds.

The Eldon title had moved away from the branch of the Scott family at Encombe, and the local public house in Kingston village duly reflected the change, with its Eldon Arms sign being replaced by that for the Scott Arms.

FORDE ABBEY

Prideaux — Gwyn — Bentham — Miles — Evans — Roper

Though lacking its Abbey Church, Dorset's otherwise most complete medieval monastery is the Cistercian house at Forde, which came to the county from Devon in a boundary swap of 1844. The parish of Thorncombe has also floated at see, ecclesiastically speaking, being shunted from Exeter diocese to Bath and Wells and then on to Salisbury. Not that any monks remain at Forde. They established Forde Abbey, at a crossing of the River Axe, in the religious revival of the twelfth century. John of Forde (1140–1214), its Abbot from 1191, came from Bindon Abbey at Wool. In elegant Latin he produced *Sermons on the Final Verses of the Song of Songs* which have remained in print across the centuries, being reprinted in three volumes by Cistercian Publications in 1977.

Forde was one of the word factories of the land. A future Archbishop of Canterbury was among its scribes. Baldwin (died 1190) had only been at Forde a year when he was appointed Abbot and had the charisma that makes for legends. As Bishop of Worcester in 1184 he heard that Gilbert of Plumpton was being executed for abducting an heiress. Baldwin rode up as the rope was in place around Gilbert's neck. He told the assembled crowd that there would be no execution on a Sunday. A royal pardon was procured for Gilbert.

Forde Abbey has lost its great church but retains most of its other medieval buildings

On promotion to Canterbury, Baldwin disappointed Pope Urban III who found he had an impetuous prelate, and monks tried to prevent his creation of what became Lambeth College. Henry II supported Baldwin whom Urban

denounced as 'the most fervent monk, the zealous abbot, the lukewarm bishop, the careless archbishop.'

The last Abbot, Thomas Chard, extended Forde and completed its north range of buildings in 1528. He then resisted its closure and surrender until 8 March 1539 when it was one of the last monasteries in Devon to be suppressed by Henry VIII's edict. Decay followed, leading to the complete loss of the 190-feet long Abbey church, but much survived of domestic buildings of 'incredible splendour and magnificence'. Their renaissance resulted from timely adoption by Sir Edmond Prideaux (died 1659). The Member of Parliament for Lyme Regis, he transformed Forde into an Italian-style palazzo, and became Mr Attorney-General Prideaux in Oliver Cromwell's Parliament in 1649. He stayed in post for life and his baronetcy was awarded in 1658 for 'the maintaining of 30 foot-soldiers' in Ireland.

The Duke of Monmouth stayed at Forde in 1680, on a tour of the West Country preceding his rebellion by five years, an involvement which cost Edmund Prideaux's son a £15,000 release fee after Judge Jeffreys threatened retribution. Forde passed from the family when Margaret Prideaux married Francis Gwyn in 1680. He created the gardens and was Secretary at War to Queen Anne in 1713. She disappointed him by failing to visit his Queen Anne's Room. The house was later let to the philosopher Jeremy Bentham from 1815 to 1818. John Frounceis Gwyn sold Forde to Bristol merchant John Miles in 1846. The contents were sold but the auctioneers regarded the remarkable wall hangings adorning the grand Saloon as fixtures and fittings. So, against all the odds, what can only be described as the best room in Dorset survived intact. Its tapestries were woven at Mortlake from Raphael's original cartoons for the Sistine Chapel in Rome.

Forde faced an uncertain future as the health of the surviving member of the next family, Mrs Bertram Evans, failed at the turn of the twentieth century. Freeman Roper found himself the owner in 1906, after it had been left to his wife in her cousin's will. Their son, Geoffrey Roper, lived at Forde for nearly eighty years and devoted his life to the house and gardens. As does his son, Mark Roper, who was born in 1935 and receives the active help of his wife Elizabeth.

They have three daughters. Alice, the eldest, manages the office and general administration of the 1500-acre estate. Sister Charlotte is the key presence in the gardens.

The author's visit found Mark Roper talking about his home and its history while breaking off a dozen times to answer an incessant telephone. The calls ranged from concert enquiries through to a prospective strawberry-picker about to set off from Moldavia. 'Where is Moldavia?' he asks. The best we can come up with, shortly before the Balkans fall apart, is that it lies somewhere amid the turmoil that is former Communist eastern Europe. 'You must obtain a visa to leave your own country first,' the caller is told.

Farming entrepreneur Tim Frost calls to tell us the latest about his thousand milking goats that will soon be herding around the monastic Tithe Barn. He cuts an impressive figure in the doorway. 'Tim established Childhay Manor Farm ice cream,' Mr Roper tells the author.

Such interruptions come about because Forde Abbey operates as a series of medium-scale overlapping businesses that sustain the home and its stunning surroundings in the splendour to which we expect our stately homes to perform. They have not compromised either the atmosphere or historical

Mark Roper at Forde Abbey

Tudor tapestry in what owner Mark Roper calls 'the best room in England'

imperatives. He was asked about the story of the flooded crypt and its reputed haunting after the River Axe swept through the Prideaux coffins:

My father saw a monk but I've never seen a damn thing. The floating story about the coffins is bunk because they are all in lead. Then the crypt was filled with clay, which we had to dig out – an awfully long and difficult job. They had thought that to fill it would force out the water but instead the damp came upwards and out into the house. It seems like yesterday but it must have been about 1970. That's when he discovered the statues that are now in the Great Hall, they were buried outside the Chapel wall. They still have some traces of gold paint and would have been set in niches like those on the side of Wells Cathedral.

Another exciting discovery came in 1991, in the North Undercroft, of a crucifixion wall mural. Dating from between 1270 and 1320 it is the earliest Cistercian figure-painting in England.

Outside, the gardens are superlative and took their rightful place on the edge of the popular Somerset circuit after winning Christie's 'Garden of the Year' award in 1993. That did 'a power of good' but a stately home seldom runs itself; 'This is a job from a more spacious age. My grandfather inherited with very little money but managed a style of sorts until the First World War. Then he died and an uncle was killed in a boating accident. My dad, Geoffrey, was planning to emigrate to Canada but came here instead. We are country family and buckled down to it. Opting out by giving it to the National Trust, or selling up, would never have occurred to them.'

The nature of the work is almost impossible to envisage today: 'My father drove produce to London in the 1930s. Can you image any landowner in Dorset today driving up to London at 3am, to call at Eton College, hospitals and then across the West End, making door-to-door deliveries?'

Mark Roper decided to do things differently; 'I didn't want to milk cows, which was the only way to farm around here, so I started to open the house on a regular basis. My parents didn't really welcome people but in fact it is not that intrusive. There is a watertight bulkhead between where we live and the public tours.'

Business also expanded into tree-growing for Fountain Forestry but that was hit by changing attitudes and on this Mr Roper uses virtually the same words as John Makepeace, at neighbouring Parnham: 'How can we go on like this, marauding our timber from the rest of the world? Woodlands were once valuable in themselves and economically vital, both for big trees and under-wood such as hazel, but we are throwing all that away, with schemes now for plantings which can only fail. The conservation lobby has also been dishonest in prejudicing public attitudes. Public forestry has been stopped and from producing a million trees a year for a purpose I'm now reduced to providing Christmas trees and cypress hedging.'

Hollywood has visited Forde. *Restoration* was filmed here during three weeks in February 1995, starring Hugh Grant, Robert Downey junior, Sir Ian McKellan and Meg Ryan. They also used Mapperton Manor. 'We don't just sit and wait for the next film to come along,' Mr Roper said as the phone rang yet again. 'Baroque music concerts are regular events in the Great Hall. EMI, Virgin and VDR from Cologne have used it for recordings. The acoustics either work or don't – our failure was with Decca but they brought sound absorbers that killed the atmosphere. The Chamber Orchestra of Europe, Consort of Music, King Singers, Borodin Quartet and Beethoven's piano have performed here. The piano came in 1992, after being found and restored in Budapest, with £3 million insurance and a 24-hour guard. All a bit over the top in terms of publicity but would you believe it, hardly anyone came – yet after a one-minute report on *Gardener's World* people poured in!'

Which just about says it all. The English are uncomfortable with culture but always make themselves at home in a garden.

FRAMPTON COURT

Browne — Grant — Sheridan

Built by Robert Browne in 1704, Frampton Court was enlarged in the nineteenth century by Richard Brinsley Sheridan (died 1888). The grandson of the playwright and poet, he married Marcia Maria Grant, the only surviving child and heiress of Lieutenant General Sir Colquhoun Grant of Frampton Court, in 1835.

Sheridan soon established himself at the centre of the Dorset social set and sat in the House of Commons for Shaftesbury and then Dorchester, from 1845 to 1868. His sister, Caroline Sheridan, married London barrister George Norton and embarked on a passionate affair with the Prime Minister, Lord Melbourne. The scandal threatened the Government and spurred legislation for women's rights, including the Infant Custody Act of 1839 and the 1857 Divorce Act.

The house and park were inherited by Richard Sheridan's son, Algernon Thomas Brinsley Sheridan (1845–1931) who married Mary Lothrop, the daughter of John Lothrop Motley, the author and historian famous for *The Rise of the Dutch Republic* in 1856. Motley was born at Dorchester in New England and died at Kingston Russell near Dorchester in old England while on a visit to his daughter on 29 May 1877. Motley was buried beside his wife, in Kensal Green Cemetery, London.

In 1794, Frampton Court was the seat of Francis John Browne

Frampton Court came upon hard times when Algernon Sheridan's death coincided with the economic crisis following the Wall Street crash and the house was largely demolished in 1931.

The Cattistock Hunt meeting at Frampton Court in the 1930s before demolition of the main building (right)

GAUNT'S HOUSE

Gaunt — Glyn

Gaunt's House, in wooded countryside above Hinton Martell, preserves the memory of the Dorset lands held by the Duchy of Lancaster after the death of John of Gaunt, Duke of Lancaster (1340-1399). It is much more recent, however, being erected in the jubilee year for George III and enlarged during the Golden Jubilee of Queen Victoria. Those years were 1810 and 1887. Its family name of the past two centuries, attached to an estate of 9800 acres to the north of Wimborne, came with a baronetcy that was created in 1800. The park covered 130 acres in three parishes.

The son of Robert Glyn and Frederica Harford, Sir Richard George Glyn (1831–1918), veteran of Balaclava and Inkerman and African adventurer, was Master of the Blackmore Vale Hounds from 1865 to 1884. The third baronet, he married Frances Fitzgerald of Maperton House, near Wincanton.

Their son Sir Richard Fitzgerald Glyn (1875–1960) was twice a knight. He succeeded his father as the fourth baronet of the 1800 creation, and a kinsman in 1942, making him the eighth baronet in the family's older baronetcy created in 1759. He married Edith Hilda Hamilton-Gordon in 1906.

The titles were inherited by their son, Colonel Sir Richard Hamilton Glyn (1907–1980), a barrister, who was MP for North Dorset from 1957 to 1970. Chairman of the Kennel Club and Cruft's Dog Show he served on the Commonwealth War Graves Commission and was president of the Society of Dorset Men. He married Lyndsay Mary Baker, which ended in divorce in 1969, and Mrs Barbara Henwood. The title passed to his son, from the first marriage, Sir Richard Lindsay Glyn (born 1943).

HAMMOON MANOR

de Mohun — Trenchard — Slade — Beech — Knight

Bucolic in its setting, between a farmyard and the Stour meadows, the thatched Tudor manor house at Hammoon is one of the prettiest buildings in Dorset. Its name comes from the Norman family de Mohun who preceded the Luttrells in their main seat at Dunster Castle, Somerset, and held another 13 manors across Dorset. In 1473 they were succeeded at Hammoon by John Trenchard. In the time of the Trenchards the manor was enhanced with Jacobean panelling.

The 'Fleeing Cavalryman' bought Hammoon Manor in 1818. General Sir John Slade (1762–1859) acquired his nickname in 1812 when he bolted from a near disaster against the French. He was stripped of his command and sent to Ireland for a year. Slow progress followed, towards recovering his reputation, and his baronetcy was created in 1831.

Dainty and delightful, in a rustic setting, the Tudor manor at Hammoon has been described as the prettiest house in Dorset

Manorial rights at Hammoon then passed to Rev. Giles Beech and the house became the Rectory until 1937. Wartime owner Lionel Knight spotted a splendid Hamstone reredos, almost certainly from a church in Somerset or Dorset and dating from the 1430s, lying in pieces in a builder's yard in the Home Counties. That was in November 1945. He bought it and put it in the nearby parish church which was being restored at the time. 'The strangest thing was that it was a perfect fit,' he said. 'It could even have come from here.'

This is the heart of the Blackmore Vale. The lawn slopes gently to the river which never swept up beyond the walls until the exceptional floods of 1979 which put both the manor house and church under two feet of water and reached the downstairs ceiling in Gale Cottage.

HANFORD HOUSE

Seymer — Ker-Seymer — Clay-Ker-Seymer — Livingstone-Learmonth

The Seymer family and their descendants occupied Hanford House, between the River Stour at Hambledon Hill, from the time of its rebuilding in 1604 till 1947 when it become Hanford School. The manor and parish of Hanford was chosen by Sir Robert Seymer, a Teller of the Exchequer, from the family property portfolio of the Dukes of Somerset. Sir Robert's knighthood was bestowed in 1619 and his completion of the courtyard at Hanford, to finish the quadrangle, took place in 1623.

Henry Ker-Seymer (died 1834) married Harriet, the sister of Horace, 3rd Baron Rivers. Their second daughter became the wife of Edward Denison, Bishop of Salisbury.

While visiting the Seymers, Sir Arthur Sullivan (1842–1900) composed an internationally known hymn tune, which he named St Gertrude in praise of his hostess, Mrs Gertrude Clay-Ker-Seymer. Sullivan was collaborating with W.S. Gilbert in the production of *Thespis* in a partnership which led to the Savoy operas. St Gertrude became Onward Christian Soldiers and was sung for the first time by the choir of St Nicholas Parish Church in Child Okeford, in 1871.

Hanford House remained the property of the Seymer family, in the time of Ernest and Evelyn Clay-Ker-Seymer, but was leased to Andrew and Noel Livingstone-Learmonth.

HERRINGSTON

Heryng — Herring — Williams

Lying in the Winterborne valley, immediately south of Dorchester, Herringston became the seat of the Herrings who have left their name across the county from Langton Herring on the Fleet coast to Chaldon Herring in the Lulworth hinterland. Their land at the latter location was exchanged for what became Herringston, through a deal with the Abbot of Bindon, in the reign of Henry III. This brought the family to 'Wynterboun' where Walter Heryng was granted a licence in 1337 to fortify his mansion with stone walls, crenellated battlements, and a gatehouse. It and the parish were henceforth Winterborne Herringston.

Herringston in 1857

The next owners were the Filiol family, until 1513, when the manor house was sold to John Williams of Dorchester. The family has remained in residence ever since. They built a courtyard house with a chapel on one side, in 1582, most of which was demolished in 1810, with the exception of the northern range beside its entrance. Thomas Leverton rebuilt it with a huge chamber behind a Gothic façade, built between 1612 and 1617, for Sir John Williams. Twenty-four decorated panels in the stupendous barrel-ceiling range in content from a gryphon to the arms of England but a series of Tudor 'grotesque figures' were displaced and discarded in the process.

Captain Berkeley Cole Wilmot Williams (1865–1938) fought in the Kachin Hills, Burma, in 1892 and was severely wounded in the Samana and Tirah Expeditions in 1897–98. He recovered to serve in the Boer War at the turn of the century and was High Sheriff of Dorset in 1931.

Captain Williams married the Honourable Winifred Mary Hubbard, the elder

daughter of the 2nd Baron Addington. Their son Major-General Edward Alexander Wilmot Williams (1910–94) commanded the 1st Battalion of the 60th Rifles in 1944, the 2nd Division of the British Army of the Rhine in 1960, and was General Officer Commanding Singapore Base District at the end of Empire in 1963. His turn as High Sheriff of Dorset came in 1970.

Herringston and its drive, from the gate, in the 1960s

HIGHCLIFFE CASTLE

Stuart — de Rothesay — Stuart-Wortley

Highcliffe is now the eastern suburb of Christchurch borough and Dorset county. The former Hampshire hamlet, acquired by Dorset in 1974, went up in the world when Sir Charles Stuart, 1st Baron Stuart de Rothesay (1799–1845) built the Gothic-revival Highcliffe Castle on its sandy clifftop. He needed a country seat closer to the capital than the Isle of Bute. As one of the country's leading career diplomats, Sir Charles Stuart, was rewarded with a peerage in 1825. Then the British Ambassador to Paris, he went on to be Ambassador to the Russian court in St Petersburg from 1841 until his death.

In the ownership of descendant Edward Stuart-Wortley, Highcliffe Castle again played the diplomatic card and hosted a three-week visit by Kaiser Wilhelm II,

Inland side of the Gothic-revival Highcliffe Castle on the clifftop east of Christchurch

Edward Stuart-Wortley with Kaiser Wilhelm II and German guests on the steps of Highcliffe Castle in 1907

Emperor of Germany and King of Prussia in 1906. An impetuous speech urging advocating friendship with England went down like a lead balloon with the 'volk' at home. In Dorset he raised a laugh when his motor car stuck in a ford in Millhams Lane, Kinson, and the *Bournemouth Graphic* recorded the occasion in verse:

> When in flood 'tis no place for a bloater
> Much less a nobleman's motor
> Jess Short and Bill Hicks
> Did the work of quite Six
> And, with others, they managed to float 'er.

The castle was empty, its future in doubt, when it had what might have been a fiery finale in 1960. It was left gutted, as the romantic ruin centrepiece for one of the best public parks in southern England, before rescue and imaginative restoration by English Heritage. The building now hosts exhibitions and other functions.

HURN COURT

Harris — Malmesbury

The mansion of Hurn Court, across the River Stour from Holdenhurst near Bournemouth, became the holiday home of diplomat James Harris, 1st Earl of Malmesbury (1746–1820). He was the son of James Harris (1709–1780), the author of *Hermes*, and Elizabeth Clarke who was the daughter and heiress of John Clarke of Sandford, Somerset. They lived in The Close at Salisbury. James Harris senior was described as 'a prig and a bad prig' by Samuel Johnson.

The Earl of Malmesbury and Viscount FitzHarris were created in 1800. By this time James Harris had been British minister in Berlin, from 1772 to 1776, and as Sir James Harris the Ambassador to St Petersburg for the following six years. His adroit management of the concept of Armed Neutrality was followed by a posting to The Hague in 1784. Here he intervened in Dutch politics and was instrumental in undermining republicanism in order to secure the future of the House of Orange.

After he left the Whig party he went on an abortive mission to Prussia, failing to hold the first coalition against France in 1793, but had more success with royal match-making. James Harris arranged the union of the Prince of Wales and Princess Caroline of Brunswick. The Napoleonic Wars followed his futile attempts at negotiating peace with the French Republic in 1796 and 1797. In 1777 he married Harriet Mary Amyand, youngest daughter of Sir George Amyand. He was created Baron Malmesbury in 1788 and bought Hurn Court in 1798 for sporting vacations. His triangular political life moved between Westminster days, Hill Street, Mayfair, for the night, and Park Place, Henley-on-Thames, at weekends.

Their eldest son James Edward Harris, 2nd Earl of Malmesbury (died 1841), was the Under Secretary for Foreign Affairs in the Canning Government in 1807, and later Governor of the Isle of Wight, but showed more interest in returning to the gun-room at Hurn and its 6750 acres.

His Shooting Journals catalogue a number of British rarities. The bagging of a horned owl on 23 December 1805 made his Christmas. A kite joined it on 4 November 1807. Marsh harriers were almost common; 'This species of harrier is by no means scarce here, and seldom a year passes without two or three being killed.' Bitterns were also winter regulars; for instance two were shot by the keeper in the last week of January 1810 and two by the 2nd Earl, at Dunmoor on 11 and 17 January 1832. Hen harriers were 'very common' and peregrine falcons are described as 'these destructive birds'. A hobby, however, was a rarity, and the White's thrush shot on 24 January 1828 was the first recorded British specimen.

The 2nd Earl married Harriet Susan Bateman Dashwood of Well Vale, Lincolnshire. His brothers went into the Church. Charles Amyand Harris became the Bishop of Gibraltar and Thomas Alfred Harris was a Prebendary of York.

The 2nd Earl's son James Howard Harris, 3rd Earl of Malmesbury (1807–89), entered Parliament for the Wilton constituency in 1841 and urged Sir George Grey, the Home Secretary, to revise the game laws. Lord Derby appointed Harris to his father's old ministry, making him Under Secretary at the Foreign Office, in 1852. He was back in office in the next Derby administration, in 1858, and given credit for keeping Britain clear of involvement in the Franco-Prussian War. Having told his peers that Napoleon III had 'pacific intentions' towards England, Harris was the first to recognise the French Second Empire, though he questioned the numbering in the Emperor's title. Harris also signed the Treaty of London to guarantee the territorial integrity of Denmark. He delayed and localised conflict between France and Sardinia and Austria and was Lord Privy Seal in Lord Derby's last administration and for Disraeli in 1874.

Edward James Harris, 4th Earl of Malmesbury (1842–1899) married Sylvia Georgina Stewart from County Down. He was aide-de-camp to Lord Strathnairn, as General Commanding troops in Ireland, and then to Sir Henry Barkly as Governor of Mauritius.

James Edward Harris, 5th Earl of Malmesbury (1872–1950) married the Honourable Dorothy Gough-Calthorpe, daughter of the 6th Lord Calthorpe and was the Senior Grand Warden of English Freemasons. President of the Library Association, from 1913, he was particularly proud of the art collection at Hurn which included Romneys, Canalettos and portraits by Sir Joshua Reynolds, but moved to Amyand House, Park Road, Winchester.

Hurn Court is now Heron Court School. The family name survives as the Malmesbury Park suburb of central Bournemouth. The cases of stuffed specimens, ranging from hoopoe to whooper swan and osprey to otter, were re-housed in dense rows by the Bournemouth Natural Science Society in a roomy Victorian villa in Christchurch Road, Bournemouth.

ILSINGTON HOUSE

Huntingdon — Oxford — Garth — Brymer — Duff

There is a royal scandal inside the hipped roof and William and Mary walls of Ilsington House which stands across the road from the church in Puddletown village with 24 acres of grounds laid out beyond. The house was rebuilt by the 7th Earl of Huntingdon after the Glorious Revolution in 1688. The Earls of Oxford followed and one of their daughters, Lady Dorothy Neville, enthused over the topiary in her diary. The late-twentieth-century successor is a 'Hortisculpture' by Judith Bakker of Nature's Dance.

A right royal interlude came with the letting of the property to Major General Thomas Garth, equerry to King George III, when he was organising travel arrangements between London and Weymouth. Charles Greville described General Garth as 'an ugly old devil' and the village story is that he fathered a son with Princess Sophia, the King's fifth daughter. The boy was born in Weymouth and taken to live with the Garths. Sophia died unmarried in 1848 and is buried in Kensal Green Cemetery.

The next owner brought Victorian values. Colonel William Edward Brymer (1840–1909) of the Dorset Yeomanry was the Member of Parliament for Dorchester from 1874 to 1885 and then represented the South Dorset constituency from 1891 to 1906. His son and successor was John Brymer (died 1921) on whose death the estate was sold with High Street houses going to the tenants at £120 each and three in Mill Street for £90 as a single lot. Winifred Legg told me of feudal days in Puddletown which was then called Piddletown:

Colonel William Brymer of Ilsington House, at Puddletown, in 1904

Squire Brymer was lord of the manor and lived in Ilsington House. He ruled everything and everybody. There was no private property except his. All the gardens had to be kept tidy. But no work was allowed to be done, or washing put on the line, on Sundays. There were seven gardeners and a full indoor staff at Ilsington House, including butler, footman and hall-boy. There were 21 domestic servants in Puddletown not counting the Brymer staff. Seats in the church were reserved for the Brymers and their staff and everyone stood when the family entered. The men wore silk top hats and frock coats and the ladies long skirts with six inches sweeping the ground and large hats with pinned ostrich feathers and a veil. Cottage women would give a little curtsey if the Squire or any of his family walked by.

It became the home of Penelope and Peter Duff, the wine trader, in 1977. They brought the house's art collection into the rock and pop age with an allegorical tribute to Jimi Hendrix. Dorset's distinguished Duff from the other side of the River Frome was Admiral Sir Arthur Allan Morison Duff (1874–1952) of Var Trees, Crossways. He commanded HMS *Birmingham* in the first action in which a ship sank a submarine in the Great War and was present in the actions at Heligoland Bight, Dogger Bank and Jutland.

His son, Sir Antony Duff (born 1920) went into the diplomatic service and rose from third secretary in Athens to British Ambassador in Nepal. Greater things lay ahead, running the Africa Desk at the Foreign and Colonial Office during sanctions against the white settlers in Rhodesia, and postings to Kuala Lumpur as Deputy High Commissioner in 1969 and Nairobi as High Commissioner until 1975. Then came the icing on the cake, succeeding Sir Michael Hanley as Director-General of MI5, the security intelligence service of counter-spies operating through the Cold War from Curzon House in Curzon Street, London W1.

IWERNE MINSTER HOUSE

Bower — Glyn — Wolverton — Ismay — Devine

The Talbot Inn on the main road at Iwerne Minster was named for the heraldic hound on the crest of the Bower family. Captain Thomas Bowyer Bower sold the estate that had been in his family for two hundred and fifty years, in 1876, to George Glyn, 2nd Baron Wolverton. He pulled down the neat Georgian walls of Iwerne Minster House in 1880. Iwerne, by the way, is pronounced 'Yewern'.

The replacement Iwerne Minster House was a palatial country seat, built in high-Victorian Perpendicular Gothic style, standing in grounds and parkland of 300 acres at the foot of the chalk escarpment south of Shaftesbury. It is now the main building of Clayesmore School.

By 1888 the title had passed in quick succession to the second son of the 2nd Baron's brother. Ferderic Glyn, 4th Baron Wolverton (1861–1932), married Lady Edith Amelia Ward. They sold Iwerne Minster House in 1908 to James Hainsworth Ismay (1867–1930). He had made a fortune by selling the White Star Fleet to American financier J. Pierpont Morgan (1867–1943).

The Ismay family seat, Iwerne Minster House, became Clayesmore School

Ismay's second marriage was to Muriel Harriet Charles Macdonald Moreton, the fourth daughter of Lieutenant Colonel Augustus Henry Macdonald Moreton, of the Coldstream Guards. They threw themselves into estate management and village life, notably during the Great War when Ismay kept up morale at home and abroad by sending newsletters to combatants at sea, on the Western Front and across the Middle East. Their letters back were posted

beneath the canopy of the parish pump which became known as the War Office.

Ismay's older brother was Bruce Ismay (1862–1937), chairman and managing director of the Ocean Steam Navigation Company Limited – universally known as the White Star Line – and proud owner of the thirteenth and most magnificent of a fine fleet of ships. James Hainsworth Ismay, Bruce's predecessor in the job until 1903, had coined the name Titanic.

Joseph Bruce Ismay, his full name, used to shoot on the Iwerne estate. He is better remembered, however, for the disaster of a single night on 14–15 April 1912 after telling the Chief Engineer of the liner, Joseph Bell, about the need for speed and the consequent consumption of coal. This was followed by improper interference with Captain Edward J. Smith, allegedly causing him to maintain his course and speed, despite an ice-warning. Bruce Ismay, seen more recently with Leonardo DiCaprio at his table, remains a prime player in the *Titanic* story and the major contributor to Wreck Commissioner Viscount Mersey's official report on the loss of the most famous vessel since the Ark.

Bruce Ismay, blamed as 'primarily responsible' for the Titanic disaster

Clayesmore School brought an imported name. The school was created at Winchester by Alex Devine (1865–1930). He was from Manchester and his first boys were from poor backgrounds. Creative manual tasks, such as woodwork, gardening and even printing, were encouraged as an alternative to compulsory games. The latter, however, provided him with an almost divine exit as the headmaster died while watching an inter-school rugby match from his sickroom window. His natural successor, Desmond Coke, had pre-deceased him as a result of war wounds. A later headmaster, Aubrey de Selincourt, passed on his enthusiasm for local history. E.M. King then made it a much more orthodox public school. Like so many before, born out of disadvantage, it found its future in privilege.

KINGSTON LACY HOUSE

Bankes

For the story of Kingston Lacy and the Bankes family one has to look southwards to the Isle of Purbeck and one of the greatest medieval fortresses in the land. The classical three-storey Restoration house, designed by Sir Roger Pratt, was built at Pamphill in 1663–65 by Sir Ralph Bankes MP to replace this castle at Corfe, which was demolished by order of the House of Commons, towards the end of the Civil War, in 1646.

Chief Justice Sir John Bankes MP (1589–1644) was born at Keswick, Cumberland and entered Queen's College, Oxford in 1604. By 1607, his parents 'perceiving him judicious and industrious, bestowed good breeding on him in Grey's Inn, in the hope that he should attain to preferment, wherein they were not deceived', to quote Thomas Fuller of Broadwindsor. He was called to the Bar in 1614 and progressed to Bencher in 1629, Reader in 1631 and Treasurer in 1632. He had entered Parliament in 1624, for Wootton Basset, and for Morpeth from 1628. In 1630 he was put in charge of the legal affairs of the infant Prince Charles, Duke of Cornwall, and knighted. In September 1634, on the death of William Noy, he took over as Attorney-General. He was said to exceed 'Bacon in eloquence, Chancellor Ellesmere in judgment, and Noy in law'.

Lord Chief Justice Sir John Bankes, life-size by Baron Carlo Marochetti, in Kingston Lacy House

Matching bronze of defiant Royalist Lady Mary Bankes with sword and the key to Corfe Castle, as sculpted by Baron Marochetti in 1853

Wealth followed fast and brought the Bankes family to Dorset, where it stayed until their abdication towards the close of the last century, having purchased Corfe Castle and its estate from Lady Hatton, the widow of Sir Edward Coke, in 1635. On the other side of the River Stour, between Wimborne and Blandford, Sir John Bankes bought the former manorial lands of John of Gaunt, from the Earl of Newport, which included the site of a residence of the Duke and Duchess of Somerset at Kingston Lacy.

Bankes prosecuted in the Star Chamber and was promoted to Chief Justice of Common Pleas in January 1641. He found himself torn between the interests of King Charles and those of the State in the widening schism between Crown and Parliament and disappointed key players on both sides by urging 'compromise and accommodation'. His loyalty at the end of the day was to the King, now based in Oxford, and he remained a Privy Councillor and Chief Justice until his death there on 28 December 1644, being buried in Christ Church Cathedral. His wife, meanwhile, was masterminding the heroic defence of the family fortress, Corfe Castle.

Their place in national history is writ large at Kingston Lacy. In the entrance hall there is a seventeenth-century marble bust claimed by the family to be Sir Ralph's father, Sir John Bankes, with moustache and goatee beard. He is wearing a shirt, tunic, and heavy black coat, and is placed on an integral plinth. The sculpture is in the baroque style of Alessandro Algardi (1602–54). Life-size bronze statues of Sir John and Lady Mary Bankes (died 1661), the heroine of Corfe's two sieges, stand on the stairs and flank their King. Charles I is seated above a superb panel featuring, in bas-relief, the Corfe conflict. These statues are by the Victorian sculptor Baron Carlo Marochetti, whose equestrian Richard the Lionheart, brandishing a sword, stands outside the Houses of Parliament. The trio of art-works at Kingston Lacy were commissioned by William John Bankes in 1853.

Upstairs in the Library are 31 keys of Corfe Castle, in two cases, and another item of Corfe memorabilia is displayed in a cabinet in the Drawing Room, as a reminder of the cause in which it was lost. It is an unredeemed 'I owe you' from Charles I dated 18 May 1644, in the troubled nineteenth year of his reign, for £525: 'Received of Sir John Bankes, Knight, Chief Justice our Court of Common pleas at Westminster … to be imployed for the finding of twentie horse to serve us in our warres.'

A number of the paintings were owned by Sir Ralph Bankes (died 1669) before he moved into Kingston Lacy, while sharing the continental exile of King Charles II, including that of two Spanish peasant boys eating fruit, after the style of Bartolome Murillo (1617–82), which was bought new and belonged to Bankes in 1659. Some paintings were not simply acquired for the house, those by Sir Peter Lely (1618–80) being traditionally supposed to have been painted there. Most of the smaller paintings are portraits of members of the Bankes family. Massimo Stanzione painted Jerome Bankes (1636–86) in Naples. He hangs in the Library. Van Dyck painted a pair – Lady Borlase (eldest daughter of Sir John Bankes) and her husband, Sir John Borlase. Other painters employed by the family included Dowdney, Jonson, Kneller, Lawrence, Romney, Roper and Weigall. The family motto is 'Velle quod vult Deus' (Desire what God wishes).

Sir Ralph Bankes became the elected member for Corfe Castle in Richard Cromwell's Parliament of 1658 and recovered his lands and property with the Restoration of Charles II. Ralph married Mary Brune, the daughter and sole heir of John Brune of Athelhampton Hall. The Kingston Lacy parkland that was chosen for their new mansion took its 'King's Farm Lacy' name from the medieval family of Lacy, the Lords of Lincoln. Though otherwise a typical Restoration man, the elegant and cultured Sir Ralph was unusual in reverting to country life, at a time when cosmopolitan comforts were high fashion.

Henry Bankes MP (1757–1834) of Kingston Lacy House represented the family ruin of Corfe Castle for nearly half a century, from 1780 to 1826, and then sat for one of the two Dorset county seats, until 1830. His portrait is in the Library and was painted in Rome by Pompeo Batoni in 1779, when he was on the Grand Tour. He became the spokesman in Parliament for the British Museum and published *A Civil and Constitutional History of Rome, from the Foundation to the Age of Augustus*, in 1818. He is said to have been offered a peerage, but declined, saying he preferred 'the good old name of Mr Bankes'.

Kingston Lacy House, as Kingston House, in 1818

Kingston Lacy was originally a brick house with Portland stone dressings, around the windows and doors, but the structure was considerably altered in the 1780s. It was gutted and its exterior re-faced in 1835 when William John Bankes MP (1786–1855) took over his inheritance and immediately commissioned architect Charles Barry to refurbished the entire building, insert a 30-feet wide staircase of Carrara marble, and add a dormered attic. That operation spoilt much of Sir Roger Pratt's work, which was a pity as it is his most important surviving building, and he does have the distinction of having been the first architect to be knighted. Charles Barry followed him in that, having rebuilt the Houses of Parliament with Augustus Pugin. The arms on the north front of Kingston Lacy House carry the date 1835.

On the other hand, William John Bankes contributed immeasurably to the contents of Kingston Lacy and left it abounding with art treasures. His collection of Egyptology is displayed in the Billiard Room. Famously, the 20-feet high ancient Egyptian obelisk from the Nile island of Philae, now on the lawn towards the ha-ha south of the house, was the key that, with the Rosetta stone, enabled Jean Francois Champollion to decipher the hieroglyphics in 1822. The inscriptions on the Philae Needle, copied by William John Bankes and Thomas Young, made a vital contribution to the deciphering of Egyptian hieroglyphic script.

Art connoisseur William John Bankes, painted by Sir George Hayter, when Bankes was a member of the Reform Act Parliament of 1832

A magnificent statue of Ramesses II, 3300 years old and brought to England as a treasure from Ancient Egypt, was re-discovered by National Trust workers at Kingston Lacy in 1991. It was dug up in the grounds, to where it had been relegated by an unappreciative household early in the twentieth century. 'A superb striding god was found prone and forgotten in the fernery,' the Trust reported in 1992.

These comprise the finest collection of Egyptian antiquities in any country house in the British Isles. Many were acquired by William John Bankes on his travels up the Nile between 1815 and 1821. In October 1818, on his longest journey, he was accompanied by the British consul, Henry Salt.

Earlier, with Giovanni Finati as his interpreter and guide, he had travelled through the Holy Land and into Syria where, disguised as Bedouin tribesmen, they rode into Petra. Here William made sketches and also stopped to measure forts, temples and other monuments, to produce the first plans of numerous ruins. Artists were employed to paint water-colours of the sites and terrain and to record ancient wall paintings.

Some of these, as painted plaster panels, he was able to bring home. Six are in the collection at Kingston Lacy and feature dancing girls and a musician. Twenty-five tomb stelae – inscribed memorials – were wall-mounted in the old kitchen. They are from Deirel-Medina, the village of the workmen who cut royal tombs, in the Valley of the Kings. The Billiard Room was chosen for the resurrected display with the billiard table providing an ideal flat, cushioned surface for showing off the wall paintings. The other special indoor treasure is a black basalt Roman head of Mark Antony which was found in Egypt and has been loaned for exhibitions in Oxford and Washington. Their significance has been emphasised by Harry James, the former keeper of Egyptian antiquities at the British Museum: 'This is the sole surviving English gentleman's collection from the early days, virtually intact and a monument to the instinctive, even if uninformed judgment, of one whose tastes were developed in the refined climate of Regency Britain.'

The portrait of William John Bankes, in the Saloon, is a preliminary sketch by Sir George Hayter (1792–1871) for his immense canvas of the 'Reformed House of Commons, 1833', which depicts the moment of the address to the Crown, on 5 February 1833. It took Hayter ten years to complete, the canvas which was later bought for the nation by Disraeli, as Chancellor of the Exchequer in 1858, and given to the newly established National Portrait Gallery. The studies of the individual members making up the picture are so competent, and the painting as a whole so well finished, that it ranks as the best massed-study of all time.

The 'collegiate pastor, master and patron, father of all mischief' to the young poet Byron, the art connoisseur William John Bankes was 'unusually handsome and was possessed of personal magnetism that captivated men and women alike'. The former were to cause him particular problems. In December 1833, when he sat for Dorset in Parliament, he was tried for an act of gross indecency with a soldier in a public lavatory beside Westminster Abbey. He was acquitted after a succession of notable figures testified to his good character, including the Duke of Wellington, Samuel Rogers, and Dr Butler, the Master of Harrow. Then on 3 September 1841, Bankes was committed to the Old Bailey, for indecent exposure in Green Park.

This time he jumped bail and exiled himself in Venice. He is said to have returned sometimes with shipments of art treasures for Kingston Lacy, to stand once more on the family seaboard at Studland. He died in Venice on 17 April 1855. Parliamentary consent was needed in order to bring home his body for burial in the family vault in Wimborne Minster.

The State Bedroom contains a mystery bed, made in the mid-nineteenth century, which was incomplete when William John Bankes died. It is a walnut half-tester bedstead with an elaborate headboard carved in relief with Venus,

Newly elevated roof-storey of Kingston Lacy House in 1853

Cupid and putti surmounted by a figure of Motherhood. The tester is supported on caryatids and columns carved with the Bankes arms and some bats. The foot-end has a figure of Silence flanked by angels, and a guardian angel with shields inscribed 'Custodit'. Its maker was Vincenzo Favenza, whose bills were settled by the British consul on behalf of Bankes's brother, George Bankes MP.

A hero of the Lucknow Siege in the Indian Mutiny was William George Hawtrey Bankes VC (1837–58), a Cornet of the 7th Hussars, the fifth son of the late Right Honourable George Bankes MP of Corfe Castle and Kingston Lacy who – to quote his memorial in Wimborne Minster – 'fell mortally wounded while charging a body of rebels near Lucknow, on the 19th of March, and died on the 8th of April, 1858, aged 21 years'. He had gone to India in 1857, at the age of twenty-one, and it was *The Times* correspondent, William Howard Russell, who would tell the world of his courage:

> A band of Ghazees, who issued out of an old mud fort and charged the guns and the party of the 7th Hussars covering them, had got the lad down and hacked at him in that cruel way until he was rescued by his comrades. It is perfectly astonishing, to witness his cheerfulness and resignation.

The Times went on to quote samples of his dying dialogue. 'If I get out of this, Russell,' Cornet Bankes said, 'they tell me I'll be able to go yachting, and that's all I care about. We'll have many a jolly cruise together.' He paused for a moment. 'If it please God.'

He was being comforted in the hospital of the 53rd Regiment in the Indian Imam Bara temple-palace. Russell described his injuries as frightful: 'One leg lopped off above the knee, one arm cut off, the other leg nearly severed, the other arm cut through the bone, and several cuts on the body.'

Whilst lying there he heard that Sir Colin Campbell had recommended him for the Victoria Cross. Cornet Bankes died and was buried in the churchyard of the ruined cantonment that stood close to the Hussars' camp. The award of the supreme national honour for valour in the presence of the enemy was confirmed by the Queen and presented by her, to his mother, at Kingston Lacy.

Walter Ralph Bankes (1853–1904) was described by his daughter Viola as 'one of the handsomest men of his generation. Women adored him and did their best to marry him, but in spite of his wealth and charm, he managed to remain single until the age of forty-four. He stood six feet in height, and a slightly aquiline nose added to the stamp of breeding which a long line of ancestors had given him.' He was the son of Edmund George Bankes and Rosa Louisa North Bastard from Stourpaine, and the grandson of Henry Bankes MP. Walter Bankes caused 'wild excitement' by driving the Jersey beauty and actress Mrs Lillie Langtry – mistress of the Prince of Wales – through Wimborne and took her to a service at the Minster. The dashing High Sheriff of Dorset then owned 30,000 acres and could claim as hereditary Lord High Admiral of Purbeck to have the power to board the flagship and take command of the Fleet if it should ever lay anchor off Studland.

The socialite who won the contest for Walter Bankes was Jenny Fraser. Known in Homburg as 'La Belle Anglaise', she split her time between Boston, Paris and London, and was the child of William Thomson Fraser, the British Consul in Java, and a Dutch doctor's daughter. Henrietta Jenny Fraser, on her arrival at Kingston Lacy in 1897 after the marriage, expressed the opinion that although the Bramah water-closet might have been state of the art when it was installed in the State Bathroom in 1785, modern times meant that plumbing had moved on. Her eldest daughter, Daphne Bankes, recalled in 1954: 'Without any structural alterations or additions of any disfiguring pipes my mother had added, for the everlasting comfort of the family and visitors, no less than eight bathrooms. There were no baths at the times of her marriage. In many cases she was "cunningly contriving to insert them wherever the experienced brain of the architect had failed to derive means".' Some, however, were a little too well disguised, such as the bath hidden in the window seat in the West Bedroom, which was not discovered to be a bath until 1983.

Despite his 'beguiling charm and courtesy', Viola Bankes wrote that her father Walter was subject to increasing mood swings and 'would set off without a word to America, his plans unfolded to my mother only by the unexpected sight of packed and labelled luggage'. She put this down to 'the disease which destroyed him at the early age of fifty-one.'

As well as Daphne, Viola and Ralph, Walter had three sons by his mistress, of 'almost the same age'. He would leave his mistress £40,000 and his wife £30,000. There was also embarrassment over the division of seaside property with the result that the widow had to buy it back off the other woman.

Jenny and Walter Bankes's son, barrister Henry John Ralph Bankes (1901–81), known as Ralph Bankes, was a sickly child who 'on several occasions nearly lost his life through illness and accidents'. His mother always asked Ralph to kneel before every visiting Bishop for the laying-on of hands. Oddly, Ralph and his sisters were never told of their father's death in November 1904, instead being led to believe that he was living in India. Their nanny suffered epileptic fits and according to Viola 'did her utmost to increase the fragility of my brother so as to make herself indispensable to his adoring but helpless Mama.' His 'frightful tempers' were put down to a daily diet of 'a pound of raw beef juice'.

Their mother's admirers included a succession of Germans, notably the extrovert Baron Louis de Meyer and the intense introvert Count Wolff-Metternich, the German Ambassador to London. The Kaiser and a coterie of German officers called for tea in 1907, during their stay at Highcliffe Castle, as guests of General Eddie Stuart-Wortley. Another royal cedar was planted beside King Edward VII's tree. Miniature mock-cannon pointed outwards across the ha-ha and 'the Kaiser maliciously enquired if we were preparing for German invasion.'

Ralph Bankes, the last private owner of Kingston Lacy and Corfe Castle, left both properties to the National Trust on his death in 1981

Ralph took Viola on his motor-cycle to Max Gate, Dorchester, to meet author Thomas Hardy and arrange for him to sit for the portrait painter R.G. Eves. Hardy and wife Florence repaid the compliment and visited Kingston Lacy on a couple of occasions. Other admirers, such as the brash Gordon Selfridge junior, were discouraged – particularly as he was always talking of creating a coastal extravaganza, on Hengistbury Head or at Studland – failing which he wanted to buy Corfe Castle. He could hardly be ignored as he proceeded around Dorset with an entourage of six Rolls-Royces. Viola made it clear that the family would not sell a blade of grass in Purbeck. Ellen Terry, 'the best-loved actress of our time', was much more acceptable company, arriving with Sir Albert Seymour.

Ralph Bankes, was the 'strong, silent' type according to his younger sister, who described him as 'good-looking in a fair and conventional English way'. Ralph – by his own choice – was the last private owner of Kingston Lacy House and squire of what at the end of his days were the 16,000 acres of the Kingston Lacy and Corfe Castle estates. He left them almost in their entirety to the National

Trust in its greatest ever bequest. Ownership passed to the Trust on 19 August 1982, a year to the day after his death, and included the antiquities and paintings at Kingston Lacy; all bar a token £50,000 gift to Ralph's son, David Bankes. He was effectively disinherited in a will estimated on the most conservative of probate valuations to total £23 million and, rather sadly, contacted me from London to ask me to find him second-hand books about the family and its lands to replace some of those that he had lost with the house.

Ralph Bankes went to Eton and served in the Royal Navy Volunteer Reserve where they were amused to find that as Lord High Admiral of Purbeck he held the right to command any of His Majesty's Ships that entered its territorial waters. He was High Sheriff of Dorset in 1939. With the death of his wife, Hilary, in 1966 he closed Kingston Lacy House to the public for the remainder of his life, and became a virtual recluse. He is buried towards the top end of Wimborne cemetery.

Viola Bankes, later Mrs Viola Hall, was searched out in Belgravia by John Rydon of the *Daily Express*. She was in no way disappointed at being omitted from her brother's will and pointed out that she had little use for £20 million. 'It was the best thing he could have done,' she said. 'Otherwise the house, my home for a quarter of a century, would just have fallen to pieces or caught fire. My brother lived only for himself. There had been no contact with him since he gave me away at my wedding in 1927. He never came near me, or my two daughters; never replied to any of my letters. He was a very selfish man. He just lived his own life, and didn't want to be bothered with anyone else. I didn't go to his funeral – it would have been a mockery. But I'm so relieved he did the right thing in the end.'

KINGSTON MAURWARD HOUSE

Grey — Pitt — Fellowes — Hanbury

The 'elegant and stately pile' at Kingston Maurward is said to have been re-cased in Portland stone in 1794 after the monarch, George III, took William Morton Pitt to task; 'Brick, Mr Pitt, brick.'

Kingston Maurward House was built on a low ridge above the Frome meadows at Stinsford by George Pitt of Stratfieldsaye, Hampshire, to supplant the Elizabethan residence of Kingston Maurward Manor. He acquired the manor on marrying Laura Grey and promised to provide for her in a fashion 'not unworthy of his ancestors'. Work took place on the new home from 1717 until 1720. The design may have been by Thomas Archer but a stronger case has been made for John James from Greenwich. Laura Pitt provided Dorchester with the classical Portland stone Grey's Bridge, in 1748, to take the London road into the county town.

John Pitt of Encombe House succeeded to Kingston Maurward in 1774 and created a big lake between the house and the river. His son was the philanthropist William Morton Pitt (1754-1836) who managed to spend the family's entire colossal resources on a plethora of philanthropic and entrepreneurial works. Stone-cladding Kingston Maurward 'at a vast expense' was but one of a series of projects that ended with him 'beggared'.

By the end of the nineteenth century it was the seat of James Fellowes. More Portland touches, including chimneys, followed during the ownership of Sir Cecil Hanbury MP (1871–1937) after the Great War. He also inserted marble fireplaces and the oak staircase. The house and its land became the post-war Dorset Farm Institute run by Dorset County Council.

Kingston Maurward House, as the home of John Pitt, in the 1790s

KINGSTON MAURWARD MANOR

Grey – Pitt

The original country house at Kingston Maurward in the parish of Stinsford, stone-built by Christopher Grey in 1591 on the Bockhampton side of the parkland, which was eclipsed by the building of a grand classical mansion on rising ground to the west in the reign of George I.

A shield over the main doorway, at Kingston Maurward Manor, depicts the arms of Grey impaling those of Stawell, and gave Bockhampton boy Thomas Hardy his first example of the use of Angel as a male personal name, which as a novelist he immortalised with Angel Clare. The real-life person in question was Angel Grey who married Katherine Stawell of Cothelstone Manor, near Taunton, during the time of Charles I. Her father, Sir John Stawell, held Exeter for the King and was imprisoned in Newgate.

Following the building of Kingston Maurward House, after Laura Grey married George Pitt, the Elizabethan manor became a farmhouse. In more recent times it has been a residential home for impoverished widows and was eventually divided into flats.

KINGSTON RUSSELL HOUSE

Russell — Michel — Hardy — Bedford — Motley —
Gribble — Lundbeck — Vestey — Carter

The famous Russell who descended from ancient Kingston Russell was John Russell, 1st Duke of Bedford, whose rapid rise in status arose from a call to dinner at Wolfeton House, though by that time he was living at Berwick Farm, near Swyre. Thus Berwick became a far-flung holding of Woburn Abbey. Francis Russell, 2nd Duke of Bedford, bought back the manor at Kingston Russell but Kingston Russell House became the home of the Michel family. The fourth John Michel (died 1739) added the frontage and entrance in Portland stone, about 1730, in a graceful Palladian style attributed to Francis Cartwright.

Vice-Admiral Thomas Masterman Hardy, Nelson's flag captain at the Battle of Trafalgar and the Hardy of the Hardy Monument, was born in Kingston Russell House in 1769. His parents were the tenants of John Michel's son, David Robert Michel, who left for Dewlish House. The 10th Duke of Bedford bought back Kingston Russell House for the Russell family in 1862.

Vice-Admiral Sir Thomas Masterman Hardy (1769–1839) of Kingston Russell House

A tablet erected by the Duke records the demise of the retired American Ambassador to London, while on a writing sojourn at Kingston Russell, though his biography says that he was visiting his daughter in Frampton Court at the time; 'John Lothrop Motley, Minister of the United States and Historian of the Dutch Republic, died at Kingston Russell House, 29 May 1877.' Motley's London residence was at 17 Arlington Street and he is buried in Kensal Green Cemetery.

George James Gribble (1846–1927), who married Norah Royds, bought the house in 1913 and commissioned architect Philip Tilden to restore it to its former glory. Their son, Captain Julian Royds Gribble (1897–1918) was posthumously awarded the Victoria Cross for his final action with the Royal Warwicks on the Western Front. Kingston Russell was then the home of Clough Burnell Lundbeck, William Vestey, and Hugh Carter.

LODERS COURT

de Redvers — Holles — Clare — Nepean — Colville — le Breton — Hood

The mansion in Loders village is beside the parish church. The manor house, owned by Richard de Redvers, Earl of Devon, became a Benedictine Priory after being given to the Abbot of Montebourg in Normandy. French monks arrived in Loders and it functioned as a religious house from 1100 to 1414. By then, however, it had been confiscated by Edward I, in 1325, and Richard II passed it to the Carthusians of St Anne in Coventry, in 1399. Briefly it was restored to the French, by Henry IV, but after the victory at Agincourt Henry V seized it back. This time it was transferred to the nuns of St Saviour Syon at Isleworth. The Priory at Loders was converted back to a manor house, after the general suppression by Henry VIII, following its sale to John Holles, Earl of Clare.

The present Loders Court, incorporating the remains of the Priory, was built by Sir Evan Nepean in 1799. It is a Georgian building, standing beside densely

Loders Court with a drift of daffodils in the 1960s

wooded parkland, which went with the Nepean baronetcy for another century. Sir Molyneux Hyde Nepean and Lady Nepean were the last to go into the family vault, in 1895, having died within four days of each other. Villagers point to the stone in the chancel floor, with a black border, and say a flight of steps lies below.

Rev. Canon Sir Evan Yorke Nepean (1825–1903) briefly inherited the property but did not occupy it. The title passed to Sir Charles Nepean but Loders went to his cousin, Sir Evan Colville (1836–1908), who was a knight in his own right, the honour having been bestowed in 1891 on retirement after thirty-eight years in the War Office. H.K. Colville then inherited the manor at Loders.

Loders Court became the home of Colonel Sir Edward le Breton (1883–1961) in 1921. He served as a Sapper in the North-West Frontier District of India in 1908 and fought through the Great War in South Arabia and Mesopotamia, where he commanded a field company. In 1933 he was appointed High Sheriff of Dorset.

It is now the home of Alexander Lambert Hood, 7th Viscount Hood (born 1914), a direct descendant of the famous naval line, and Diana, Viscountess Hood. Alexander Hood charted a career from Harvard Business School, through directorships at Petrofina, Schroder Wagg and Wimpey, to Charing Tanks Consolidated Investments. He also served on the British Waterways Board.

LULWORTH CASTLE

Howard — Bindon — Suffolk — Weld — Weld-Blundell

A mock-castle, rather than a fortified building, Lulworth Castle was conceived by Thomas Howard, 3rd Baron Howard of Bindon (died 1611). With rounded towers at each corner and a balustraded terrace above its wide flight of steps it was finished off by William Arnold as a castellated hunting-lodge in 1609. In 1605, however, the unfinished building was sold to Lord Thomas Howard, 1st Earl of Suffolk (1561–1626) who had distinguished himself in action against the Spanish Armada and was appointed joint Lord Lieutenant of Dorsetshire in 1611.

Rubble came from the ruins of Bindon Abbey, or both Bindon Abbeys as they are at Lulworth Cove and Wool, and bricks as well from Mount Poynings which was the nearby home of Sir Thomas Poynings. The Weld name arrived with Humphry Weld, from a Catholic family in Cheshire, who bought Lulworth Castle in 1641. He was the grandson of the Humphry Weld who was Lord Mayor of London in 1609. Charles II and James II came to stay at Lulworth.

Humphry Weld (1611–85) brought the family to Dorset

Impotent squire Edward Weld (1705–61) married the Honourable Catherine Elizabeth Aston, Lord Aston's daughter, in an arranged marriage between the two powerful Catholic families. The relationship soon failed and in 1731 husband and wife were in the Arches Court at Canterbury where the bride had filed a suit for nullity on the grounds of Weld's impotency. He had undergone treatment for a physical abnormality and was able to defend the case successfully. A secondary issue was of Catherine's libel in bringing the original action and this also went her husband's way.

The nation was able to snigger at the pair in pamphlets on *The Cases of Impotency and Virginity Fully Discuss'd, The whole of the proceedings in the Arches Court* and *A sequel to the Case*. Eighteen letters between the former couple were published. Catherine went home to Staffordshire, where she died in 1739, which released Edward Weld to marry Teresa Vaughan in 1740. She redeemed his reputation the following year with the first of five children. The eldest son, Edward, is renowned as the first husband of Mrs Fitzherbert who went on to contract a clandestine marriage with the Prince of Wales, later George IV.

Edward Weld senior employed the Bastard brothers from Blandford to install marble fireplaces between 1740 and 1756 as well as re-vamping the general decoration with the plaster mouldings of Georgian fashion, as did his second son, Thomas Weld, who brought Pompeian flourishes to the Upper Drawing Room and also re-decorated the Dining Room. The four-poster Royal Bed, designed for frequent visitor King George III, had a domed canopy, gilded crest, and royal blue hangings. The Palladian temple-like Catholic Chapel, the first Roman Catholic church built in England since the Reformation, was built in the grounds in 1786. Thomas Weld founded the Catholic College at Stonyhurst and was father to Humphry Weld of Chideock Manor, to the yachtsman Joseph Weld and to Cardinal Thomas Weld (1773–1837) of Lulworth Castle who invited French Trappist monks to East Lulworth in 1796. He was then married to Lucy Bridget Clifford. Their only child was Mary Lucy Weld who had been born at Upwey in 1799.

James I made the first royal visit to Lulworth Castle

After his wife died, at Clifton in 1815, Thomas Weld reconsidered his life, and when his daughter married her second cousin, who became the 7th Baron Clifford, he was free to enter the Catholic ministry. The family property he

Sir John Weld (1615–74)

Mary Stourton (died 1651), wife of Sir John Weld

Edward Weld (1705–61) whose early death was to have more significance than his life

Maria Anne Smythe (1756–1837), widow of Edward Weld, went on to marry the future King George IV

Thomas Weld (1750–1810)

renounced in favour of his next brother, Joseph, who became one of the foremost Victorian yachtsmen.

Thomas was ordained priest in 1821 and worked at first in Chelsea and Hammersmith. His rise in the ecclesiastical ranks started as Bishop Coadjutor of Kingston, followed by consecration as Bishop of Amycla, Canada, in 1826. In 1830 he arrived in Rome and was told a few hours later that Pope Pius VIII was to honour him with the purple, as the second Englishman to be admitted to the College of Cardinals since the death of Cardinal Howard, in 1694. Back at Lulworth, exiled King Charles X of France, found a refuge in the upheavals of 1830, before moving on to a safer haven in Scotland. Cardinal Weld lived in the Odescalchi Palace and is buried in the church of S. Maria Aquiro.

His brother, yachtsman Joseph Weld (1777–1863) of Lulworth Castle, dominated the Cowes event in the mid-nineteenth century. His series of winning

vessels included *Alarm*, *Arrow* and *Lulworth*. He was one of the founders of the Royal Yacht Squadron.

Joseph's second son, Thomas Weld, was secretary to his uncle, Cardinal Thomas Weld, and also succeeded to the Ince Blundell estates in Lancashire in 1837. His nephews Reginald Joseph Weld (1842–1923) and Humphry Joseph Weld (1854–1928) died without issue so his son, Herbert Joseph Weld, inherited in 1928. It was during his tenure that the mansion was gutted by fire in 1929.

The Prince of Wales with Princess Caroline of Brunswick (with Pekinese) and George III (with walking stick) and the Queen, visiting Lulworth Castle in about 1800

Joseph Weld (1777–1863) designed and skippered racing yachts

The Drawing Room, Lulworth Castle, in 1917

Lulworth Castle ablaze on 29 August 1929 with rescued items from lower rooms being gathered on the lawn

Neighbouring landowners Lieutenant-Colonel Sir Joseph Weld (centre) and Major-General Mark Bond (behind him), at Broadmayne, as president and vice-president of Dorset Community Council in 1987

On Herbert's death in 1935, the estates passed to his first cousin once removed, Colonel Sir Joseph Weld (1909–92). The commander of the 4th Battalion of the Dorset Regiment from 1947 to 1951 he then became High Sheriff of Dorset. He was Lord Lieutenant of the county from 1964 to 1984 and chairman of Wessex Regional Health Authority. The family seat, built to replace the gutted castle, in the parkland at East Lulworth, is Lulworth Manor.

❦

LYTCHETT MATRAVERS MANOR

Maltravers – Trenchard – Watts – Carrell – Cecil

One of the lost country houses of Dorset, the Manor House at Lytchett Matravers was demolished after the Second World War, succumbing to a fatal attack of woodworm and dry-rot. With it went one of the last direct links with Dorset's regicide though his family name survives in the names of three south-east Dorset parishes. The other two, in the Isle of Purbeck, are Langton Matravers and Worth Matravers.

'The Maltravers Fret' is the memorial brass in Lytchett Matravers parish church to Sir John Maltravers who died in his seventies in 1364. That he died in his bed in peaceful old age was remarkable, given that he had at an earlier time fled England into exile and been 'sentenced by Parliament to be drawn, hanged and beheaded as a traitor for compassing in the death of the Earl of Kent'.

His major contribution to English history, however, was what he did to the Earl of Kent's brother, the homosexual King Edward II in 1327. Sir John Maltravers and William Burney assassinated the monarch in Berkeley Castle, Gloucestershire. The regicide was carried out with the most outrageous barbarity. Edward was held down on a table and had a red-hot poker inserted into his rectum – 'sleyne with a hoote broche putt thro the secret place posteriale,' to quote a contemporary chronicler. The method of the killing had two points in its favour. Firstly it left no mark that would be noticed and therefore enabled the body to be put on view to support their claim that the King had died naturally. Secondly it appealed to the participants as appropriate revenge for Edward's sexual proclivities.

The King was succeeded by his fifteen-year-old son, Edward III, but only in name as the country was effectively governed by the late King's widow, Isabella, and her lover, Roger Mortimer.

The brass to Sir John Maltravers was rediscovered in 1924 when some pews were lifted. In 1972 I drew the attention of the rector, Rev. James Mahon, to the fact that it was being scuffed by chairs and the pianist's feet. 'I had better see to this and move the chairs,' he said. 'It used to be covered by coconut matting and I will see what I can do.' Mr Mahon added that if there are any remains of Maltravers's body they would be in the Trenchard vault under the church floor, 'which has been sealed for the past fifty years'. One day, he hoped, he might have an opportunity to explore down there.

The notable Trenchard from the Manor House at Lytchett Matravers was Sir John Trenchard (1640–95) who moved on and bought Bloxworth House.

Various families followed and the final occupants included John Watts at the turn of the twentieth century and Colonel T.B.H. Carrell a generation later. For memories of Manor House ghosts and servants, I was directed towards veteran villager Matilde Jane Cox (1868–1975). She died at her home, Seaview in Foxholes Road, shortly before she was due to celebrate her 107th birthday. Dorset's oldest inhabitant had spent all her life in Lytchett Matravers and embodied local continuity, dying in the centenary year of its school which she attended as a first-year pupil on the day it opened in 1875. Her children went to the same school. Then her grandchildren. Great-grandchildren Trevor Hunt (aged five) and Tina Hunt (aged ten) were attending it at the time of her death.

Mrs Cox recalled the building of Lytchett Heath House, an Elizabethan-style mansion east of the village, in the same year as she started school. It was erected for Lord Eustace Brownlow Henry Gascoigne Cecil whose London home was in Eccleston Square.

MAPPERTON HOUSE

Brett — Morgan — Broadrepp — Compton — Labouchere — Montagu — Sandwich

The sandwich as a snack pre-dates the noble family's arrival in Dorset. Mapperton, in a fold of Dorset's western hills between Beaminster and Maiden Newton, was the replacement for Hinchbrooke in Huntingdon,

The rambling setting of front and back buildings at Mapperton

Viscount Hinchingbrooke, MP for South Dorset, renounced the title Earl of Sandwich in order to remain electable as Victor Montagu

in 1955. As for Sandwich in Kent that was merely the token place of the title – a redundant Cinque port after the Royal Navy had moved along the coast to Portsmouth. That more desirable name was no longer available as a title. 'Otherwise we would be munching "portsmouths",' John Montagu, 11th Earl of Sandwich (born 1943) quipped to me, at Mapperton House.

The 4th Earl invented the concept of fast-food when he called for meat between two slices of bread, so that he could snack at the table instead of deserting a promising hand during an all-night card game. 'We are thinking of creating a millennium sandwich in the gardens,' his descendant told me in 1996, by which time Britons were spending £5.2 million each day on ready-made sandwiches. 'Our bread for topiary is yew, with box for the filling.' Not that edible, one would think. 'That won't stop the deer,' Caroline Montagu interjected. 'They keep eating great swathes through the roses, which are definitely their favourite.'

The family was brought to Dorset by Victor Montagu, 10th Earl of Sandwich (1906-95), who was the Conservative MP for South Dorset from 1941 to 1962. He then held the title Viscount Hinchingbrooke and had something of a reputation for lost causes, ranging from the post-war Purbeck campaign for the release of Tyneham from Army occupation, and opposing the military adventure at Suez, through to what became three decades of masterminding national opposition to British involvement in the Common Market and its European Community successor. On inheriting the earldom he renounced it under legislation brought about by Viscount Stansgate, the Right Honourable Anthony Neil Wedgwood Benn, and since known as Tony Benn.

The origins of Mapperton lie with the Brett and Morgan families, from the time of Edward I, with the Morgan griffins having been carved for Robert Morgan who rebuilt the house between 1540 and 1560. In 1618 it passed by marriage to

Richard Brodrepp. His son, also Richard Brodrepp, built the ranges of stables and 1670-dated coach-houses that face each other across a courtyard. The third Richard Brodrepp was succeeded by the fourth who rebuilt the north front in about 1755 and died in 1774. Catherine Brodrepp, his daughter, married John Compton of Minstead Manor, Hampshire in 1788. Henry Francis Compton was his descendant there at the turn of the twentieth century. Mrs Labouchere was the owner between the Comptons and Viscount Hinchingbrooke.

The 1st Earl of Sandwich, who gave us the noble sandwich, with his successor

MELBURY HOUSE

Sampford – Folior – Maltravers – Bruning – Strangways –
Fox – Ilchester – Fox-Strangways

The parish with Melbury House at its heart is named Melbury Sampford for the family that held it in the thirteenth century, before a succession of marriages took it through the Folior, Maltravers and Bruning families.

Sir Giles Strangways (died 1547), who rebuilt Melbury House, was one of King Henry VIII's Commissioners who undertook the suppression of the religious houses, which gave him first pick of their estates. He bagged the Benedictine Abbey at Abbotsbury with the Chesil Beach and its hinterland due south of Melbury. Horace Walpole described Melbury as 'a sumptuous old seat in a fine situation' across the low hills north of Evershot. Most distinctive is the hexagonal 'lofty and fresh tower' which Sir Giles raised from the middle of the west side of the courtyard. Wonderfully carved over-mantels in the original eastern entrance hall were attributed by Walpole to Grinling Gibbons.

The next Sir Giles Strangways was succeeded by Colonel Sir John Strangways (1584–1666) who married Grace Trenchard. He spent a period in the Tower of London after the surrender of Sherborne Castle in the Civil War. Sir John's grandson, Thomas Strangways (1643–1713), brought classical touches as he progressively rebuilt the frontages of the house.

Founding father of the Ilchester dynasty at Melbury was Sir Stephen Fox, a stalwart supporter of the exiled King Charles II, and then the key figure in the founding of Chelsea Hospital. His son, Stephen Fox, was created the 1st Earl of Ilchester in 1756. The 1st Earl's daughter, Lady (Christian) Harriot Fox,

Melbury House, from across the lake, in 1905

Seaward second seat, Strangways Castle, overlooking the Chesil Beach (foreground) at Abbotsbury, in 1857

became Lady Harriot Acland (1750–1815) on marrying John Dyke Acland, the eldest son of Somerset landowner Sir Thomas Acland.

Lady Elizabeth Talbot, the eldest daughter of Henry Thomas Fox, 2nd Earl of Ilchester, was the wife of W. Davenport Talbot of Lacock Abbey, Wiltshire. Their only son, Henry Fox Talbot – who died in 1877 – discovered the technique of modern photography. The 2nd Earl died in 1802 and his widow, Maria, Countess of Ilchester, was appointed a supernumerary Lady of the Bedchamber by Queen Charlotte in 1804, and was in attendance at the Queen's death. Lady Ilchester died at Abbotsbury in 1842.

The Duke and Duchess of Gloucester visited Melbury House in October 1817. Harry Fox-Strangways, 3rd Earl of Ilchester, died in 1858. Lady Theresa Strangways, eldest daughter of the 3rd Earl, was one of the train-bearers to Queen Adelaide at the coronation of William IV on 8 September 1831. In 1836, she was appointed Lady-in-Waiting to the Duchess of Kent and then, after marrying, she was Woman of the Bedchamber to Queen Victoria, until 1856 when her husband succeeded to the title Earl of Digby. Theresa's younger sister, Lady Caroline Strangways, who married Sir Edward Kerrison, described the Queen's appearance at a ball in 1842; 'The Queen's dress was not becoming, and she looked hot and oppressed. It was a heavy crown with gold things coming down on each side of her face. Prince Albert's dress was magnificent, and very becoming. He was, I think, the best dressed person there. He had a sort of embroidered tissue, or cloth of gold, which cost 15 guineas a yard, and which was so brilliant that all his other jewels and diamonds were quite eclipsed by it. He personated Edward III.'

The Ilchester Arms, topping off the Ilchester Arms Hotel, at Abbotsbury

William Fox-Strangways, 4th Earl of Ilchester (died 1865), was a distinguished diplomat. As the Honourable William Strangways, he moved around Europe from St Petersburg to Constantinople, The Hague, Florence, Naples and Vienna. In 1835 he was appointed Under Secretary of State for Foreign Affairs, when Lord Palmerston was Foreign Secretary, and was the Envoy Extraordinary to the Germanic Confederation from 1840 to 1849. His brother, the Honourable John Fox-Strangways also led an exciting life, and accompanied the Honourable Henry Anson, fifth son of Thomas, 1st Viscount Anson, in an espionage expedition across the Middle East. They dressed as Arab pilgrims and set off from Alpello to Mecca, but were seized and imprisoned, in 1827. The French consul secured their release but Henry Anson had contracted the plague and died as a result. John was put in quarantine and eventually returned home to Melbury.

Henry Edward Fox-Strangways, 5th Earl of Ilchester (1847–1905), succeeded his uncle in 1865. The son of the Honourable John Fox-Strangways, he married Mary, the only daughter of the 1st Earl of Dartrey. Apart from a year as Captain of the Honourable Corps of Gentlemen-at-Arms, in 1873, he devoted his life to managing his immense estate of 32,900 acres which had Melbury House as the main seat, Abbotsbury Castle and Gardens as its seaside villa overlooking the Chesil Beach, and a spacious third home at Redlynch House in parkland near Bruton, Somerset. His London residence was Holland House and his clubs were the Carlton, Turf, Travellers' and White's.

Giles Stephen Holland Fox-Strangways, 6th Earl of Ilchester (1874–1959), was also Baron Ilchester and Strangways, Baron Ilchester and Stavordale, and Baron Redlynch. He served in the Coldstream Guards and was appointed Chevalier of the French Legion d'Honneur in 1918. He married Lady Helen Stewart, the only daughter of the 6th Marquess of Londonderry, and together with the Countess of Ilchester researched and published the *Life and Letters of Lady Sarah Lennox*. He then edited the *Journal of Elizabeth, Lady Holland*, whose home provided his London residence, being Holland House in Kensington. Having compiled the chronicles of the house, and written a life of Catherine the Great, he applied his skills as a biographer to his family and their extensive network of friends. Subjects included the Honourable Henry Edward Fox, Sir Charles Hanbury-Williams and Lord Hervey.

Edward Henry Charles James Fox-Strangways, 7th Earl of Ilchester (1905–64) was the eldest son of the 6th Earl; he served in the Second World War in the Royal Horse Guards and outlived both his sons.

The Princess of Wales (Princess Victoria Mary of Teck) with Lady Stavordale, at the Ilchester Arms, Abbotsbury, on 8 December 1904

As a result, Walter Angelo Fox-Strangways, 8th Earl of Ilchester (1887–1970) was from another branch of the family and inherited the title a month before his seventy-seventh birthday. He had served in both wars, first in intelligence and then with the infantry, and was a London businessman, who fondly followed football fortunes though 'unfortunately no longer a participant'. The earldom was now detached from its historic seat, with the Earl living in Torquay.

His son, Group Captain Maurice Vivian de Touffreville Fox-Strangways, 9th Earl of Ilchester (born 1920), lived in Westerham, Kent, and became President of the Society of Engineers in 1974.

MELCOMBE HORSEY

Turges — Horsey — Freke — Pitt — Pitt-Rivers — Woodhouse

The ancient manor of the Turges family in the centre of the county passed to the Horsey family of Clifton Maybank by marriage and inheritance in the reign of Henry VIII. Nearly a century later Sir George Horsey married a daughter of Sir Thomas Freke (died 1633) of Shroton and mortgaged the estate to her father, who moved in and gave it Jacobean panelling and plaster ceilings as well as a private chapel.

Melcombe Horsey, across the valley from Bingham's Melcombe, in 1857

Ownership passed to the Pitts and Pitt-Rivers as gentrified residency moved sideways. Much of the old building survives, including a fine wagon roof,

stone bellcote and carvings of Tudor roses and the crowns of England and Scotland. The old house still gives its name to the parish, Melcombe Horsey, though it is now much better known for its other seat, Bingham's Melcombe.

Higher Melcombe, as it is now known, is the home of John and Marjorie Woodhouse of the brewing family from Blandford which grew out of the local Ansty Brewery and provided soldiers throughout the twentieth century. They included the wartime Commandant of Blandford Camp.

Lieutenant-Colonel John Woodhouse, formerly of the Dorsetshire Regiment, joined elite forces in the Malayan insurgency and went on to command 22 Special Air Services. He devised the first week-long survival selection course in Snowdonia, triggering a bout of malaria, but returned to re-take it and pass. From the bare mountains of Oman, where he saved the Sultan of Oman from desert guerrillas, he went on to the tropical jungle in Borneo. There, in 1964, Jock Woodhouse devised 'shoot n'scoot' tactics for cross-border operations by deep penetration patrols armed with Armalite rifles. 'Those bloody ghosts' were ordered to leave nothing behind. Not a single cigarette stub, cartridge case, or footprint of a standard-issue military boot.

Brigadier Charles Woodhouse was the first member of the county regiment to win the Military Cross, at Trousvilles in 1914, and completed his military career as Colonel of the Dorsetshire Regiment from 1946 to 1952

MELPLASH COURT

de Melplash — More — Paulet — Brodrepp — Gundry — Tiarks — Buckler

The manor house in 40 acres of parkland on the eastern side of Netherbury parish retains its pedigree in its name and that of the hamlet beside the main road from Beaminster to Bridport. The de Melplash family were followed by Mores from Marnhull, notably Sir Thomas More (1478–1535), Lord Chancellor of England, though his residences were Crosby Place, Bishopsgate, followed by 'The Great More House' at Beaufort Row, Chelsea, and country estates in Oxfordshire.

Melplash passed to Thomas Paulet, the second son of the Marquess of Winchester, and the family held it until 1693. It was then bought by Richard Brodrepp and became one of the farms on the Mapperton estate for more than two centuries. Rebuilding was carried out by Mrs Gundry, of the Bridport rope-making family, in 1922. P. Tiarks followed and it is now the home of Penelope and Robert Buckler.

MERLEY HOUSE

Constantine — Ash — Willett — Adye — Hamilton —
Rodney — Wimborne — Hambro

The former thatched Willett Arms between Wimborne and Gravel Hill has been replaced by a twentieth-century roadhouse. Willetts Bay is on the north-west coast of the island of St Christopher, now known as St Kitts, in the West Indies. The two locations, separated by thousands of miles of sea, owe their link to Ralph Willett (1652–94), the eldest son of Henry Willett and Martha Robinson who married in London in 1649.

St Christopher had become the second English settlement in the Caribbean, in 1623. Barbados was the first, in 1605, and Ralph Willett probably sailed there before moving to the smaller island. By that time, in 1675, it was divided between the English and the French. The latter held the extremities, north and south, and the English settled along the narrow strips on each side of the central hinterland. This rose towards the 3800-feet summit of Mount Misery, an extinct volcano, and all lay in an active earthquake zone which was also regularly visited by tropical storms. Raids were also frequent in Ralph Willett's time, both from native Caribs and piratical Spaniards, and life was literally on the edge in terms of terrain and topography.

It was also a place for making or losing a fortune. Interest continued from the Old World, both from adventurers and politicians, with the latter finding such places a convenient dumping ground for criminals and subversives, including those transported from the West Country in the aftermath of the Duke of Monmouth's rebellion in 1685. Tobacco, from Virginia, had been the first cash-crop in the colonial plantations but by 1644 it was eclipsed by sugar. Historian Alan J. Miller surmises that Ralph found land increasingly at a premium on Barbados and transplanted himself to the 'Wild West' colony of St Christopher where there was much less competition for fertile volcanic slopes.

By 1678 he must have been doing quite well, as his younger brother Captain William Willett had sailed out to join him, as they were then inhabitants of Trinity Point parish in the south of the island. Ralph married Anne Estridge, the daughter of planter John Estridge, and became Speaker of the Island Council.

Their sons, Henry and John, married sisters Elizabeth and Mary Stanley. They were the daughters of Colonel John Stanley from the sister island of Nevis which had been settled by the English from 1628.

Colonial tensions erupted. The French captured the English garrison in 1669 but Christopher Codrington, the Governor of the Leeward Islands, re-took the island in a three-week campaign in 1670. Ralph Willett died in 1694 and Henry and John expanded their holdings after Christopher Codrington junior had thrown the French off St Christopher in 1702. The French eventually found an opportunity to retaliate, in 1706, landing to burn every plantation, as the English took refuge in Fort Charles, and the compensation claims resulting from this incident confirm the presence and status of the Willett family. A total of 334 English planters registered losses of £145,000 with the Plantations Office in London.

Alan J. Miller examined these documents in the Public Record Office and found that Mrs Margaret Willett valued a brass candle-stick and snuffer at 4s-6d, but he soon realised that colonial living was quite spartan: 'Life on these tropical islands was in fact far from paradise – with a frightfully high mortality rate from nutritional and hygienic disorders.'

France ceded ownership of St Christopher to England in 1713 under the Treaty of Utrecht. In 1729, having lost his wife Elizabeth in her next child-birth, Henry Willett decided that their two young sons, Ralph Willett (1719–95) and Henry Willett, should be sent to England. They were dispatched in the care of Captain William Harris of the *King George*.

Money followed them home. Ralph Willett inherited a total of 21 West Indian plantations on his father's death in 1740. Henceforth he was phenomenally rich, establishing the family's town house in Dean Street, and then buying the Merley estate in Dorset from William Ash in 1751. Its manor house, Merley

Hall Farm, now stands on the south side of the Wimborne by-pass which has cut it off from a virtual riverbank situation beside the Stour. It had been in the hands of the Constantine family until Harry Constantine died in 1712 and is a delightful warren of a building with an accumulation of parts from different periods including a core of seventeenth-century brickwork and an oak staircase with bulbous balusters. There is some surviving panelling.

Ralph had the cash to do better, between 1752 and 1759, with Merley House being reconstructed as a three-storey rectangular building, basically in brick with Portland stone facings. The work was undertaken either by provincial builder Francis Cartwright or the Bastard brothers from Blandford. The major classical flourish is at the centre of the north facade where the steps rise from each side between temple-like Doric columns that are surmounted by a pediment.

The real elegance is inside, with rococo plaster decoration to the walls and opulent scenes from classical mythology moulded into panels for the ceilings. Ralph Willett made himself very comfortable. In 1764 he became a Fellow of the Royal Society. The south-facing main room on the ground floor at Merley House, 'designed for a Saloon', became a library as he amassed an enormous collection of books. These were the reason for the two wings being added to the house in 1772, with the eastern one being a purpose-built Library. Its bookcases stood 13 feet high and the ground-floor room itself was nearly twice that height and width, and 84 feet in length. Its matching western partner was the Art Gallery. These two-storey wings were linked to the house by curving corridors.

In the Caribbean, France having ceded ownership of St Christopher to Britain under the Treaty of Utrecht in 1713, returned in 1782, though the island was retaken by the Royal Navy the following year.

Ralph was safe in England, and seems to have remained in Britain for the rest of his life – no longer regarding himself a 'Kittifonian' – during which time he married a couple of London widows but produced no children of his own. He therefore befriended and adopted a cousin's erudite son as his heir. Ralph died in Merley House on 13 January 1795 and was buried in the family vault in the churchyard at Canford Magna. There is a memorial above the chancel arch.

The chosen beneficiary, John Willett Adye, was an active contributor to intellectual London society, initially as a member of the convivial Society of Dilettanti, and was then elected to the prestigious Society of Antiquaries in 1800. He was required to change his name, becoming John Willett Willett, but entered the rolls of the Antiquaries as John Willett Adye, which was obviously how he was known. Ralph Willett's other legacies benefited friends, hospitals and several clusters of cousins back in St Christopher. They were probably grateful that cash was flowing in the reverse direction, having suffered a hurricane in 1772 and reduced sugar harvests as a result, followed by increasing competition from Cuba and Brazil, and regional turmoil as the Americans declared themselves independent in 1776.

Decline at home was just as dramatic. John Willett Willett disinherited his son John, who was behaving increasingly oddly, and the family had him declared insane in 1808. He was removed to Broomhall at Shooters Hill, Kent, where he survived until 1839. Meanwhile, John Willett Willett refers rather ominously to 'the present circumstances of my family' in 1811 and was taking the hot mineral waters in Bath to try and revive his health. The vultures hovered over Merley and descended on its corpse in 1813. The extensive Library and matching Art Gallery at Merley House were emptied of their contents in 1813 and raised in excess of £13,000 and £7000 respectively for the collection that had been Ralph Willett's pride. Then – having lost their purpose – these two wings of the great house were demolished and John Willett Willett died, still in Bath, in 1815.

Alan J. Miller's research for his article in issue No. 92 of *Dorset – the County Magazine* shows the extent to which the family fortune in the West Indies depended on Afro-Caribbean slavery. Slavery was outlawed in the British Empire by an Act of Parliament in 1833 and its implementation in 1835 was mitigated, for families like the Willetts of Merley and the Draxes of Charborough, by a £20 compensation package administered by the Colonial Office. There were hundreds of slaves in the ownership of the various branches of the Willett family on St Christopher. In 1817, a census listed 244 of them, ranging in age from Great Sue (aged sixty-nine) who drove the 'Grass Gang', to a young Stanley 'who does nothing yet'. By 1822 the number had risen to 261 and at the end of the era, in 1835, there were 351, valued at £15,370.

The Merley estate, of 1600 acres, passed to barrister Henry Ralph Willett – brother of the unfortunate John – who had chambers at Old Square, Lincoln's Inn. He died, unmarried, in his rooms at The Albany, Piccadilly, in 1857. The holdings in St Christopher were still part of his estate and they and Merley were inherited by a distant relative.

Willett Lawrence Adye was the son of Henry and John's cousin, Major James Pattison Adye, of the Royal Artillery. Being from a military family, the beneficiary was also on the War Office pay-roll, but Miller traces this to a non-combatant role: 'Clerk Third Class in the Department of the Director of Stores and Clothing.' He was living in Blomfield Street, Paddington, before being propelled into the life of a country gentleman at Merley, where he presided over further decline and fall. The estate was sold in 1875 and he died in 1878, leaving a widow, Elizabeth, who died in Parkstone in 1906.

Merley was briefly home to the Duke of Hamilton and then Lady Rodney. It then provided a last home for Cornelia, Lady Wimborne from Canford House, and Captain Angus Valdemar Hambro, who was born at Milton Abbey.

MILTON ABBEY

Tregonwell – Damer – Milton – Dorchester – Portarlington – Hambro

John Tregonwell (1625–80) who from the age of five was a legend throughout his lifetime

Founded as a Benedictine house by King Athelstan in 934, the present Milton Abbey dates from 1322 to 1500, with massive rebuilding having been necessitated by a lightning strike and fire in 1309. It came into private hands, those of Sir John Tregonwell (circa 1498–1565), during the Dissolution of the Monasteries, in 1539.

As Commissionary-General at the Court of Admiralty, he was talent-spotted by Henry VIII and propelled into the diplomatic theatre. He negotiated for England in the Netherlands and then secured two peace treaties with Scotland. He then helped in the sequence of personal proceedings against the Carthusians, Sir Thomas More, Anne Boleyn, and in the matter of the King's divorce of Katherine of Aragon. Above all, he took the surrender of the monasteries, with Milton Abbas being but one of the opportunities of which he took advantage. Though he often complained of receiving 'little reward' from the

State he emerged a rich landowner, and was eventually knighted, in 1553. John Tregonwell, Sir John's grandson, inherited Milton Abbey. His grandson was the next significant member of the family.

Look up at the south side of the tower of Milton Abbey and you will see the location and scale of what was acclaimed as a miracle. Aged five, the fifth John Tregonwell (1625–80) was standing on the parapet with his nanny, in 1630, when he embarked on one of life's little adventures. John leant over to pluck a rose that was growing from the stonework. He lost his balance and toppled off his perch, falling a hundred feet, to the lawn below. Here he continued to indulge his love of flowers and proceeded to pick the daisies.

John owed his life to the high fashion of the day for little boys – a buckram-lined nankeen pinafore – which billowed like a parachute and gave the child a slow-motion descent. He went on to become High Sheriff of Dorset and built the magnificent stone fireplace in the Abbot's Hall. He bequeathed his library to the church in 'thankful acknowledgement of God's wonderful mercy'.

Feudalism in its most extreme manifestation has left a landscape legacy at Milton Abbas, Middleton as it was known, where an entire medieval town was swept away and replaced by parkland with a neat double row of look-alike cottages around the corner in an adjoining valley. Dorset's major inland tourist attraction was built at the whim of Joseph Damer, 1st Lord Milton and 1st Earl of Dorchester (1717–98), who bought the former Milton Abbey and its lands in 1750. He was impressed with its potential as a grand private house but became increasingly irritated and infuriated that all the noises and smells of the bustling town of Middleton were present around the clock on the other side of the garden wall. They included at close proximity the already famous Milton School, the George Inn and King's Arms just beyond, and then the remainder of a densely-packed town stretching for a mile down the valley.

Boys being boys, the school proved to be the last straw, with its lads clambering across his lordship's roofs to drop stones down his chimneys, and other pranks against blatant manifestations of wealth and authority. At the less interesting end of the list of offences came the inevitable annual outbreak of apple and pear scrumping. Such things were an excuse for what became an obsession. Joseph Damer wanted a great house that re-asserted itself into the setting and a park that would be the envy of his peers.

He resolved to rid himself of the insanitary huddle of a town that extended down the High Street, up Newport Street, and forked into Back Street on the east side of the valley, and along Broad Street and Duck Street to the foot of Fishway Street beside the stream and the monks' old fishponds. Damer envisaged all this swept away and replaced by a great lake.

He put the vision into effect, by building two dams, and literally drowned out the last reluctant inhabitant, but the underlying chalk geology partially defeated his grand gesture. The permeable strata caused his plans to leak. The lake stabilised at its present level and its western dam became an unnecessary causeway, leading to what is now one of the public school dormitories. The lake did, however, succeed in its prime purpose. In the lower part of the town it covered the sites of houses in depopulated Back Street and Broad Street. The Harrison family were the last to leave a little further up towards Milton Abbey. The ousted population was largely displaced and dispersed. Middleton had ceased to exist.

The favoured few who were to be retained as estate workers were rehoused around the corner, out of view, up a side valley known as Luccombe Bottom. As a disincentive to 'idleness and drinking' they had no public house. They were, however, provided with their own parish church in a model village of matching thatched cottages which was to be known as Milton Abbas. Milton Abbey, henceforth, was relieved of this purpose and became the private chapel to Damer's adjoining home in Abbot's Hall which was re-clad for him as a mock-Gothic mansion to plans by John Vardy and Sir William Chambers. On the south side of the courtyard, Abbot Middleton's Great Hall still survives, from 1498.

Dr Richard Pococke, visting in October 1754, expressed pleasure; 'Lord Milton is casing it all round in a beautiful modern manner.' Sir William Chambers, however, was less than impressed with the designs that were forced out of him for 'this vast ugly Gothic house' by its 'unmannerly imperious lord, who has treated me, as he does everybody, ill.'

James Wyatt was commissioned for the new Adam-style interiors. Elegant marble fireplaces were designed by Thomas Carter and carved by Richard Westmacott senior.

The Jacobean double wings of banded flint-and-brick of the Almshouses, facing northwards at the junction of Broad Street and Newport Street, midway between the present lake and Milton Abbas, were brought in cart loads to a site opposite the new church of St James which was being erected by the nation's top architect, James Wyatt, between 1774 and 1786. The Jacobean Almshouses in Middleton were endowed by Jane Tregonwell in 1674 for 'six poor widows'. On their re-erection in Milton Abbas, in 1779, they were given an ornate Romanesque centrepiece featuring Lord Milton's arms, above an entrance leading to what was a public reading room.

Joseph Damer, contemplative in the after-life, in marble at Milton Abbey

The creator of this landscape, Joseph Damer, was created Lord Milton in 1753 and Earl of Dorchester in 1792. Six years later he died of 'a gruesome disease' and is preserved in weary cupped-hand resignation as a superb life-size marble effigy in his Abbey. His daughter-in-law was one of the remarkable women of her age. Anne Seymour Damer (1749–1828) had Horace Walpole as her childhood mentor and philosopher David Hume as the friend who reproved her for laughing at an Italian street sculptor; 'You could not do better.'

She almost immediately set about proving him wrong, first with a wax model of a head, and then made her first stone bust. The future sculptress of high society – who presented Napoleon with a bust of politician Charles James Fox – worked under Ceracchi, Bacon and Cruickshank. She married John Damer, the eldest son of Joseph, in 1767. He was the heir to a fortune of £30,000 a year, but set about spending it prematurely. When the combined minus figure of John and his two brothers reached £70,000, with father Joseph refusing to meet the debt, John Damer shot himself following a liquid supper 'with a blind fiddler and worse company' at the Bedford Arms, Covent Garden, on 15 August 1776.

Captain Lewis Tregonwell, descended from the Tregonwells of Milton Abbey, whose seaside retreat at Bourne Mouth, in 1810, earned him the epithet 'Founder of Bournemouth'

The 2nd Earl of Dorchester was without an heir and the estate passed to his sister, Lady Caroline Damer. She was a confidante of the royal family, from being a bridesmaid to the Princess Royal on her marriage to the Hereditary Prince of Wurtemberg Stuttgart in 1797, when residing at Dorchester House in Park Lane. On her death in 1828 she bequeathed Came House, another of her properties, to Colonel the Right Honourable George Lionel Dawson Damer, third son of the 1st Earl of Portarlington. His second son, the Honourable Henry Dawson Damer, lived in Milton Abbey, with his wife, Eliza Moriarty. Their only son, Henry Dawson Damer, 3rd Earl of Portarlington, succeeded his uncle, the 2nd Earl, in 1845. They were the Irish branch of the family.

Joseph Damer's replacement Milton Abbas, no longer visible from Milton Abbey

The first significant addition to facilities in Milton Abbas, breaking Damer's tee-total edict, had been the conversion in the 1820s of the thatched former slaughter house, in a long thatched building towards the top end of the village street. It became the Portarlington Arms.

The street at Milton Abbas, now a tourist attraction, in 1970

The 4th Earl of Portarlington, who had married Harriet, daughter of the 6th Lord Rokeby, sold Milton Abbey estate, with its 8600 acres and five villages including Milton Abbas, in 1852. The buyer was Baron Hambro and the Portarlington Arms instantly moved with the times and became the Hambro Arms. It was supplied with village-brewed ale, from Fookes Brewery at the bottom of the street, until 1950 when it was bought out by John Groves of Weymouth.

The Hambros were at the top of the national banking pyramid. Baron Hambro's son, Sir Everard Alexander Hambro (1842–1925) was Director of the Bank of England. His third son, Captain Angus Valdemar Hambro

King Edward VII (centre), surrounded by Hambro family and friends, in the woods above Milton Abbey

Milton Abbas estate sale particulars of 1852 offering 'the splendid mansion' and 'beautiful old Abbey'

(1883–1957), travelled the world for a year and met his future second wife, Vanda Charlton, in Malpas. An old Etonian, he played golf for England and cricket for pleasure, and went into Parliament. From 1910 to 1922 he was the Conservative member of Parliament for South Dorset and then the National Unionist member for North Dorset, before and during the wartime coalition, from 1937 until 1945. He saw junior ministerial service, as Parliamentary Private Secretary to the Under Secretary for Air, in the closing two years of the Great War. He was High Sheriff of Dorset in 1934–35.

Shortly after this, while living at Merley House, near Wimborne, he found himself the unwitting contact in a chain of typhoid bacteria traced by Dr Vernon Shaw from Froude's Dairy, Bournemouth, back to unpasteurised milk and cows drinking from a drainage ditch below the house. There the farmer's wife had become dangerously ill and died of the disease on 8 September 1936. More than 700 people contracted typhoid fever and 51 of them died in the worst outbreak in Britain since Victorian times.

The ultimate irony at Milton Abbey, which must have Joseph Damer turning in his grave, is that from 1953 – when it was under threat of demolition – his home has been overrun by the 275 boys of Milton Abbey School. There is no longer aristocracy in residence in either fold of this double valley.

In London, Damer's prestigious home was Dorchester House, in Park Lane. It remained part of the Milton Abbey estate until 1852, and the sale by Lord Portarlington. Bought by R.S. Holford, it was rebuilt in 1857 to Italian Renaissance plans, by Lewis Vulliamy. It was the architect's principal work in the capital (out of town it is Westonbirt House) but was pulled down in the 1920s to make way for a replacement building. This is the Dorchester Hotel.

MINTERNE HOUSE

Churchill – Digby

The ancient seat of the Churchills and the Digbys saw them linked again in marriage in October 1939 when Randolph Churchill, the son of Winston, married Pamela Digby. Randolph was replaced by Leland

Hayward, followed by American diplomat Averell Harriman, and it was as the Honourable Mrs Pamela Digby Churchill Hayward Harriman that the daughter of the house ended up serving her adopted country as United States Ambassador to Paris.

Minterne House was originally the Manor of Cerne Abbey. After the Reformation it passed from Winchester College to the first Sir Winston Churchill. He enlarged the house and left it to his younger son, General Charles Churchill, which infuriated John Churchill, 1st Duke of Marlborough, whom destiny had provided with Blenheim Palace at Woodstock, Oxfordshire. General Churchill's widow died in a fire in the family's town house in South Street, Dorchester, which now houses a bank. Admiral Robert Digby bought Minterne House and much of the Cerne valley, from her executors. He regarded Minterne as ill-contrived and ill-situated and described the location as 'bare'. He planted shelter belts to lessen its exposure to the elements, at the 650-feet contour above the head of the valley, between hills rising to 850-feet.

Lord Digby describes its evolution from downland into parkland; 'This landscape is entirely man-made, different from those hills that stretch from here to Dorchester, and was shaped during the peace dividend that occurred between the American War of Independence and the Napoleonic Wars. Ships were laid up and officers sent home on half pay.'

The family's most evocative war relic is a battered copy of Milton's *Paradise Lost* which was on the table in Captain Digby's cabin in HMS *Africa* at the Battle of Trafalgar. A French cannon ball passed between it and a Bible as its owner, who survived to be Admiral Sir Henry Digby (1770–1842), was clearing the deck for action. The crew ditched 105 bags of bread, two casks of beef, three of pork, one cask each of oatmeal, suet and sugar, ten butts, seven puncheons, 12 hogsheads, and ten cases of lemon-juice. They then sustained 63 killed and wounded in going through the French line and came through the other side as a fine ship 'cut to pieces but sound in bottom'.

Naval battles became incorporated into family names. Edward St Vincent Digby, 9th Baron Digby (1809–89), was the son of Admiral Sir Henry Digby and Lady Andover, who succeeded his first cousin once removed, Edward, 8th Baron and 2nd Earl Digby (1773–1856). Edward's mother was Jane Elizabeth, Viscountess Andover (1777–1863), the widow of Viscount Andover and eldest daughter of Thomas William Coke, 1st Earl of Leicester (1754–1842).

The only daughter of Sir Henry Digby and Lady Andover was Jane Digby, Lady Ellenborough (1807–81). Edward, 1st Earl of Ellenborough – described as rich, vain and imperious – was seventeen years her senior, and Jane's 'dazzling grace and charm' soon saw her moving through fast society and falling in love with Prince Swartzenberg. She was divorced from Lord Ellenborough by Act of Parliament in 1830 and went into overseas exile in exchange for 'pin-money'.

More high-profile love affairs followed as she travelled through the Balkans and Middle East. Her second divorce was from Baron Vennington. After two years of studying Arabic, at the age of fifty-two, she married twenty-seven-year-old Medjuel el Mazrab. He was a chief of the Anizee Bedouin and Mrs Digby – as she was known – went with him across the desert to Damascus and Baghdad. 'An intermarriage with an European, it is true, is the one new thing under the Sun to them,' she wrote home, 'but I am very popular amongst them, and adopt their customs, dress and manners.' Leading 'the ordinary life of an Arab's wife' she wore the traditional blue robe and ground corn, milked camels, washed her husband's hands and feet, and cooked his food and waited on him while he ate it. 'I am bare legged as the rest, only as my feet have not

'That is John Digby, who brought us to Dorset,' Lord Digby explained

Lord Digby's second son, Rupert, looks just like first Dorset ancestor John Digby

'Shivered' is the word for the spine of this shot-damaged book salvaged by Henry Digby, Nelson's youngest captain, from HMS Africa at the Battle of Trafalgar

Young Digbys in the art gallery at Minterne House

The ostrich is the emblem of the Digby family and the motto 'By God, not by luck'

yet attained the desirable state of horn necessary to trot over the flints and thorns, I am allowed a pair of yellow boots.'

Edward St Vincent Digby married lady Theresa Fox-Strangways, daughter of Henry Stephen Fox-Strangways, 3rd Earl of Ilchester. Their eldest son, Colonel Edward Henry Trafalgar Digby, 10th Baron Digby (1846–1920), of the Coldstream Guards, sat in Parliament for Dorset from 1876 to 1885 when he sailed on the Suakim expedition. In 1893 he married Emily Beryl Hood, daughter of the Honourable Albert Hood, of that other naval lineage.

Military life and horses also appealed to their eldest son, Colonel Edward Kenelm Digby, 11th Baron Digby (1894–1964), who won the Distinguished Service Order, Military Cross and bar, and Croix de Guerre during the Great War. He was Master of the Cattistock Foxhounds from 1926 to 1930 and President of the Royal Horse Show and numerous horse-breeding, cattle improvement, veterinary and agricultural societies. He married the Honourable Pamela Bruce in 1919. Their eldest son rounds off the current succession and is the source for this potted account of the Minterne story.

Lancelot 'Capability' Brown came to Dorset and 'spent the day at my favourite ploy' as he put it. This was 'cascading' which was how they described the art of making weirs and waterfalls, with lakes forming behind them. His employer in Dorset was Admiral Robert Digby's brother at Sherborne Castle. 'Robert went to lunch there and picked his brains,' Lord Digby told the author. 'The result was 14 cascades at the top of this valley.' Cedars were planted. 'Sadly, all those 200-year-old trees were accounted for in the January gale of 1990. I put the damage down to the drought of the previous year having loosened their roots. It was a combination of things.'

The Minterne branch of the Digby family have always been keen gardeners. Lord Digby puts this down to the vagaries of geology and location. 'There is a mound of greensand down the middle of the valley. That is mixed with two centuries of leaf mould. You couldn't grow a single rhododendron a hundred yards to either side. My brother, who was a real plants-man, said he was growing a jungle and that it needed to be that – because they cannot stand without support all round them.'

Many of its plants are rarities. As well as receiving imports of recent discoveries, Theresa Fox Strangways, who became Lady Digby, went to the High Himalayas to bring back new species. More came as a result of the Kingdon and Ward expedition to Sikhim and Nepal in the 1920s. Below there is a changing carpet of colour with snowdrops, aconites, viburnum, and wild garlic. The badgers have a taste for the latter.

The present Minterne House, replacing the ancient pile, was built by architect Leonard Stokes between 1902 and 1905. Sir Edwin Lutyens, who went on to design the Cenotaph, was one of his pupils. Stokes specialised in churches and telephone exchanges. His renewal of Minterne House was characteristically strong and assertive in a straight and solid no-frills style with a great square tower of the sort that often disguises Edwardian water-tanks. 'I'm extremely grateful to him,' the present Lord Digby says of Leonard Stokes. 'Before the war there were 14 indoor servants. Then it was used as a Naval hospital. After the war my mother couldn't see how you could run the house without lots of servants. Big old houses were having to go into the stately home business, but that is quite a rat race, and anyway we no longer had the historic fabric to show off, or to have to repair.' The alternative was to put two-thirds of the great house into flats. 'It was designed to all face south, so it's a long house. We cut off our end, so they have their own entrance and drive. What we've got left is

Minterne House in 1964

large and we are able to have lots of concerts and other things. It is open for special parties for friends of charities and events I host as Lord Lieutenant. We have lots of interesting pictures, which tell quite a story historically, but are not what the art market would regard as "good" in the investment sense.'

Pamela Digby's brother Edward Henry Kenelm Digby, born 24 July 1924, is the 12th Baron Digby in the Irish line, created in 1620, and 5th Baron Digby in the English succession, created 1765. A painting and a photograph tell the story of the family, as Lord Digby pointed out, for they are identical: 'That is John Digby, who brought us to Dorset. That's my second son, Rupert. How alike they are – 400 years of genes.'

Lord Digby, known to his friends as Eddie, went from Eton and Trinity College, Oxford, to a military career on the outbreak of the Second World War. He returned to conflict in the post-war Malayan insurgency and left the British Army of the Rhine during the Cold War, to marry Dione Marian Sherbrooke, the daughter of Rear-Admiral Robert St Vincent Sherbrooke VC. Their son and heir is the Honourable Henry Noel Kenelm Digby who was born on 6 January 1954.

Steps into parkland below the square tower of Minterne House in a balanced creation by Edwardian architect Leonard Stokes

The 1939 marriage between Pamela Digby and Randolph Churchill delighted the latter's father who came to Minterne House as First Lord of the Admiralty, after visiting Portland Harbour, and returned as Prime Minister. A painting from his wilderness years is the closest that the house's art collection comes to impressionistic works. Lord Digby is particularly proud of the Churchill connection: 'He was delighted with the marriage. All the Churchills and the

Painting in Minterne House, by Winston Churchill in 1934, from his 'wilderness years' which ended in 1939 with events un-related to the marriage of son Randolph and the Honourable Pamela Digby

Spencers were descended from George Digby, Earl of Bristol. We had the old Churchill home here and all descended from a minor line of the family, and they brought us to Dorset.'

MORETON HOUSE

Frampton — Frampton-Hobbs

'Father of the turf' Tregonwell Frampton (1641–1727), born beside the River Frome at Moreton House, near Wool, trained horses at Newmarket. He bet on a colossal scale, but with the knowledge that generally enabled him to win: 'He made as light of throwing away £500 or £1000 at a time as other men do of their pocket-money, and was perfectly calm, cheerful and unconcerned when he had lost a thousand pounds as when he won it.' Between races he went hawking. He also managed the royal stables, and his memorial stone records he was 'keeper of the running horses to their sacred majesties William III, Queen Anne, George I and George II.'

Fir Hill Obelisk, a 70-feet spire with a 10-feet high urn standing on top, protrudes in Portland stone from the wood half a mile south of Moreton House. It commemorates James Frampton (died 1784) who rebuilt the parish church in 1776 and was pre-eminent in the development of the estate and its house. The building dates from 1742–44 and has a main classical wing of Portland stone to a ground-plan 70-feet square. James Frampton's hilltop monument was erected by his friend Captain John Houlton in 1786 and was designed by James Hamilton of Weymouth. At the base, facing the house, was a Latin inscription on a white marble tablet, with the English translation on the opposite side overlooking Winfrith Heath.

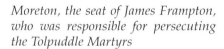

Moreton, the seat of James Frampton, who was responsible for persecuting the Tolpuddle Martyrs

These inscriptions were later moved, descendant in residence Commander R.H.C. Frampton told the author in 1974: 'In the late-nineteenth century, the tablets were removed owing to damage done to them by persons trespassing and were placed in the wooden portico in the village, opposite the old school, which formed the entrance to the kitchen gardens. These tablets were again moved when the portico was badly damaged by an Army vehicle in 1954 and are now to be found just inside the entrance to the cemetery.'

The Duke of Gloucester, the brother of King George III who first visited Weymouth in 1789, came to Moreton to shoot when 'pheasants were so plenty, royalty was much less common, and the fuss and attention paid were considerable.'

James Frampton's son, Lieutenant-Colonel James Frampton (1769–1855), Commandant of the Dorsetshire Yeomanry Cavalry, achieved lasting notoriety as a magistrate in 1834, by initiating prosecution of six members of the Friendly Society of Agricultural Labourers. They were known at the time as the Dorchester Unionists but became the Tolpuddle Martyrs after eventual pardon and release in Australia from penal transportation. Frampton married Lady Harriot Strangways, the third daughter of Henry Thomas Fox, 2nd Earl of Ilchester, from Melbury House. From 1814 until her death in 1817 he was a close friend of Princess Charlotte, sailing with her from Weymouth on *The Royal Charlotte*, and taking the royal party on excursions from Portland to Corfe Castle, often concluding with dinner at Moreton. A lock of the late Princess Charlotte's hair was placed in a brooch and attached to the belt which the Princess presented to Lady Harriot Frampton at the Royal Lodge, Weymouth, on Christmas Day in 1815. It was brought to Moreton by the Princess's husband, Prince Leopold of Saxe Coburg, during a stay in Weymouth. Princess Charlotte had died while trying to deliver him a son. Frampton's epitaph reads: 'Sincere in his religion. Upright. Honoured. Beloved.'

His sister, diarist Mary Frampton (1773–1846) lived in Moreton House until 1786, and had posthumous fame when her jottings were published as *The Journal of Mary Frampton*. This fascinated Victorians with its lush picture of high fashion and country-house living, interspersed with visits to London and court anecdotes both from there and the royal travelling circus to Weymouth, plus touches of fear when prestige and power were threatened by the mob. She was in Town during the Gordon Riots and at Moreton during the Captain Swing fires of 1830. She displays high Toryism, a strong will and capacity for observation, but there is the standard feminine interest in weddings and the general social round. Paradoxically, though she was at the centre of the county's social set, Mary would never marry. She moved with her mother, Phillis Frampton (1737–1829) to Wollaston House (now called Agriculture House) in Dorchester, where the parties went on as before. Mary Frampton's niece, Harriot Georgina Mundy, prepared the journal for publication in 1885.

Prince Clarence (1835–49), the second son of the King of the Mosquitoes, died whilst being educated in England and is buried at Moreton. His homeland was in central America, in Belize and the islands of the Bay of Honduras, where the friendly connections between the natives and the British caused resentment in Washington and disputes with the United States.

Framptons remain at Moreton with Richard Frampton-Hobbs living in the family mansion.

MOTCOMBE HOUSE

Whittaker — Grosvenor — Westminster — Stalbridge

Before gentrification, Motcombe House was known as Palmer's Place and was the home of William Whittaker, until his death in 1816. Its progress up the social scale began in 1825, as a sporting estate for Richard Grosvenor, 2nd Marquess of Westminster, of Grosvenor House, Park Lane, and of the family that owned 30,000 acres of Cheshire and Flintshire and was and is one of the wealthiest in the land.

The mansion of his second son, the 1st Baron Stalbridge (1837–1912), is red-brick with Hamstone dressings and was built in 1894 at a cost of £160,000, to designs by architects George and Peto in 100-acre grounds between Gillingham and Shaftesbury. His son, Hugh Grosvenor, 2nd Baron Stalbridge (1880–1949) served as a Lieutenant in the 14th Hussars in the Boer War and won the Military Cross in the Great War. He had no heir and the title died with him.

Motcombe House is now Port Regis School and the Grosvenor riches have moved sideways. With an estimated worth of £4,400 million, Gerald Cavendish Grosvenor, 6th Duke of Westminster (born 1951), held number one position in *The Sunday Times* 'Rich List 2001'.

PARNHAM HOUSE

Gerard — Strode — Hody — Sprat — Oglander — Robinson —
Sauer — Rhodes-Moorhouse — Bullivant - Makepeace

Thomas Sprat, from Parnham House, became Bishop of Rochester and Dean of Westminster

The magnificent Tudor mansion of Parnham, a mile out of Beaminster at the foot of the hills beside the Bridport road, now houses the art-carpentry workshops of the John Makepeace Foundation. It was built in about 1400, by the Gerard family, and expanded into its present imposing state during the subsequent 250-year reign of the Strode family. Their leading males showed a talent for attracting heiresses who brought dowries which allowed Parnham to flourish.

One such was Elizabeth Hody, grand-daughter of Henry VII's Lord Chief Baron of the Exchequer, Sir William Hody, whose marriage to Robert Strode (died 1558), in 1522, brought the fortune that enabled Robert and their son, John Strode (died 1581), to rebuild Parnham. Forgetting the later pinnacles, theirs is the east front and its splendid porch. As for the south and west fronts, the renowned architect John Nash reconstructed them, in 1810, not that they are pure Nash either. Vincent Robinson, Parnham's owner from 1894 to 1910, embarked upon his own 'De-Nashionalisation'. I would like to know whether he also coined the pun; particularly as his efforts pre-dated Britain's short socialist experiment by forty years. Either way, I love the phrase, and the gems he inserted into the Nash facades. These include stone mullioned windows from Wroxham Abbey – he discarded the neo-Gothic wooden ones – which bring proper style to the dining room in the west front.

They are complemented by stained glass from Nonsuch Palace, Cheam, which is contemporary with the stonework that Nash pulled down. Inside there is a link with Sir Walter Raleigh, in the form of linen-fold panelling taken from his bedroom at West Hawsley Place. This lines the Oak Room.

The east front of Parnham House in 1857

The abrasive dean of Westminster Thomas Sprat (1635–1713) was born in Parnham House. His father, the town clergyman, had married one of the Strode daughters, and their son never lost his appreciation of 'hospitality beyond his purse'. Sprat championed science, writing the *History of the Royal Society of London*, and is remembered as a poet. Politics, however, were nearly his downfall, but he survived accusations of conspiring to restore the exiled monarch James II and delivered *A Sermon Preach'd to the Natives of the County of Dorset* at the 'anniversary feast' of Dorsetmen in London in 1692.

The King's Room is where Charles II slept on a visit to the Strode household. The family became extinct a century later, despite Sir John Strode's nine sons and four daughters, from two marriages. The last of the male line was Thomas Strode (died 1764). Only the last child, a daughter named Elizabeth, produced surviving children. She had married into the Oglander family, from Nunwell in the Isle of Wight, and Parnham passed to Sir John Oglander, though they chose to rent it out until Sir William Oglander made it his home at the turn of the nineteenth century and commissioned fashionable John Nash to rebuilt it.

The last of the Oglanders at Parnham died in 1896 and the house came on the market for the first time in its history – previous changes of ownership had always been by inheritance or marriage – and the buyer was art expert Vincent Joseph Robinson (1829–1910). The author Sir Arthur Conan Doyle (1859-1930) came to stay with him. The story is that his sleep was disturbed by a howling dog and that this gave him the idea for the *Hound of the Baskervilles* which was published in 1902. Vincent Robinson provided Beaminster with its Market Cross in The Square, in memory of Elizabeth Julia Robinson in 1906. She was his sister; Robinson never married. After his death Dr Hans Sauer gave Parnham a swift restoration from 1911 to 1913.

Lieutenant William Barnard Rhodes-Moorhouse of Parnham House won the Royal Air Force – then the Royal Flying Corps – its first Victoria Cross

He was followed on the eve of the Great War by a wealthy widow, the Maori mother of pioneer aviator William Barnard Rhodes-Moorhouse, who had been the first to fly through the Golden Gate in San Francisco and to carry passengers across the English Channel. His more lasting fame came with his death at the age of twenty-seven on 27 April 1915. He died on the Western Front, from wounds received in bombing Courtrai, having taken off at 15.00 hours on 26 April in a BE-2b biplane, from Merville, to drop a 100-pound bomb on a railway bridge over the River Lys in German-occupied Belgium.

To do so he flew at 300 feet through a hail of bullets, mainly unleashed from the church belfry, but the bomb hit its target – temporarily tearing-up the track. Rhodes-Moorhouse and the BE-2b were equally shot-up but limped back to Merville. There the flyer was resigned to his fate, with massive gunshot wounds to his thigh and abdomen, and survived only twenty-four hours.

Such was the admiration of his commanding officer that he implemented William's request that his body should be shipped home to Dorset – itself a rare honour as it was a wish denied to almost all the other dead heroes – and another tribute followed. William Barnard Rhodes-Moorhouse had won the Royal Flying Corps (and therefore the Royal Air Force) its first Victoria Cross.

Parnham House, south side, shadowed by John Makepeace

He left a widow, Linda, and a baby son, William Henry Rhodes-Moorhouse, who was born in 1914 and followed his father's example in the next war by winning the Distinguished Flying Cross for 601 (County of London) Squadron in the Battle of Britain. At its peak, on 6 September 1940, his Hurricane was shot down near Tonbridge, Kent. His ashes joined his father's remains in the same Parnham plot. Linda had lost her husband and son at the same ages and from the same cause. She had already moved on, and Edward Bullivant

bought Parnham in 1930, with the next big change coming in 1955 when it was converted into a residential home under the auspices of the National Association for Mental Health. They created a refuge for confused and distressed old ladies which closed in 1973.

Parnham would be on the market in time for John Makepeace's second coming to Dorset. He arrived first as a student in 1957 to learn cabinet-making with Keith Cooper in the Old Chapel at Lytchett Matravers. Having turned down offers of Oxford he was back there a decade later having been commissioned to furnish the new wing of Keble College. His remarkable creative talent had already won worldwide acclaim and exhibitions followed, in London's New Art Centre and the Victoria and Albert Museum, and then on the international circuit.

Next he was head-hunted by Lord Eccles for the Crafts Council; 'That was intended to improve the lot of artist craftsmen. It was a further catalyst as I realised the benefits of integrated and intensive residential courses. Travel in the States had shown me that there was a need for broader education that was not just training in techniques and crafts, but combined with business and marketing skills. No one else was doing that.'

There are limits to the creative vision of quasi-autonomous non-governmental bodies, and the Makepeace exposition demanded an example rather than a dream. Awaiting it, in the deep green valley south of Beaminster, was Parnham. In 1976 it had been on the market for three years, during the seemingly endless property recession, after the collapse of house prices. For £100,000, reduced to £70,000, Parnham offered abundant space. One hundred rooms, I guessed. 'Sixty-five in fact,' John Makepeace answered, 'but quite a few are the size of a normal house.'

For fourteen years it had been in institutional use. The ancient fabric was reasonably well maintained but planners were anxious that one of Dorset's most splendid Grade One historic buildings was being left empty and vulnerable to vandalism or worse.

John Makepeace was its saviour and the following year, after raising a further £100,000 for furnishing and equipment, the operation was declared to be up and running. 'Things went crazy,' Mr Makepeace recalled. 'We had the stu-

Art rennaissance at Parnham with furniture designer John Makepeace at one of his own tables to a Crawford Adamson backdrop

dents arriving and no building.' They found just one working room, upstairs in an outhouse, which was hastily transformed into a functioning workshop. Eleven Makepeace disciples came and went off into work to create their own reputations. Similar numbers followed each year, including Lord Linley who brought media interest, and a visit from the Duke of Edinburgh to glisten the cachet of royal approval.

Makepeace modernity coexists with flagstone floors and elegant period settings. Phoenix II, a chair, rises from the ashes, factually in that all its materials – such as holly and burr-elm – are those normally discarded on the woodsman's fire. It complements rather than contrasts with the backdrop of the fireplace in the 1535-built and John Nash re-tuned Great Hall, beneath the 'Never Vanquished' arms of Dr Hans Sauer. The essence of Makepeace design is that it is naturalistic, exemplified by the chair with nine reed-maces as its back, almost rustling in a warm summer breeze. Another, with rustic legs and patterned three-dimensional leaves for the seat, looks as if it has materialised from a Walt Disney cartoon. The wood is carved to celebrate what the designer describes as 'its life-force, the tree'.

Chair in leaf, typifying John Makepeace's avant-garde design

The Makepeace philosophy is to liberate craftsmen to copy nature, and to encourage connoisseurs to appreciate their work and take it into their homes, coupled with practical experiments in ecologically-sensitive applications in Hooke Park which the Parnham Trust bought from the Forestry Commission in 1983:

> For years craftsmen have been aping machine precision and blandness. They have also copied the form and expression of other materials. The English were spoilt by the availability of large and larger colonial trees. Forests overseas were not planted but mined. We are running a research programme into the use of thinnings and so-called second grade timber. The house designs we come up with will offer solutions and influence attitudes. People need to have it demonstrated – and at Hooke this is possible – that building regulations can be interpreted to give them approval. Engineers devise radical structures and the architects wrap them. Architecture has gained too high a profile and is regarded as superior to engineering, which is demeaning.

The comedians Eric Morecambe and Ernie Wise are commemorated with twice life-size bright blue fibre-glass statues in the trees immediately north-east of Parnham House. The sculpture is by Nick Munro and was for the British Genius Exhibition at Battersea Park in 1977. It was then placed in Regent's Park but removed after public petitions that they were too 'vulgar'.

POST GREEN

Bond – Lees

Post Green was built as the late-Victorian residence of Henry Pomeroy Bond. In the twentieth century it became the second home of the Lees family whose main residence, South Lytchett House, stands in the park across the road at Lytchett Minster.

Sir John Victor Elliot Lees died in 1955 and was succeeded by his second son, Sir Thomas Lees (born 1925), as fourth baronet. During the war he lost an eye while serving in the Royal Air Force. He married Faith Justin Jessiman in 1949. Their evangelical and social works around the estate included Lytchett Minster Gospel Association and Post Green Community Trust. Sir Thomas Lees was High Sheriff of Dorset in 1960 and a member of the General Synod of the Church of England from 1970. His heir is Christopher James Lees (born 1952).

Sir John Lees of Post Green (left) with Edward Tory, joint masters of the South Dorset Hunt in 1949

POXWELL HOUSE

Howard — Henning — Trenchard — Lane

Poxwell was known as Pokeswell in the Middle Ages and that is how its inhabitants, such as Major Mick Burgess, still pronounce it. Its manor was a property of Cerne Abbey. After the suppression of the religious houses by Henry VIII, Queen Elizabeth granted Poxwell manor to Thomas Howard of Lulworth Castle. He sold Poxwell in 1575 to Poole merchant John Henning, whose family were among the first of the new rich to reach the top of the social pinnacle, providing a Sheriff of Dorset in 1609.

By 1613 the Hennings had rebuilt and enlarged Poxwell House and they continued in residence until the nineteenth century. They had been linked by marriage to the Trenchards of Lytchett Matravers and Wolfeton from 1699 and that prolific line – still socially active across Dorset into the third millennium – eventually secured Poxwell. Its last distinguished Henning was Weymouth banker Edmund Henning who frequently entertained King George III at the house. For this he was rewarded with a royal loving cup in 1800. It travelled with descendants to Australia and was in the proud possession of Edmund Thomas Henning of Newcastle, New South Wales, when tracked down in the edition of *Country Life* for 5 September 1936.

John Trenchard Trenchard, in 1868, built a neat Gothic church at Poxwell, dedicated to St John the Evangelist, to replace what was described as 'a Saxon church' but it too has since been demolished. His roadside conduit, the parish pump, has fared better and is dated 1843.

After the departure of the Trenchards, Poxwell Manor became the home of Ernest Lane, from Bloxworth House.

POYNTINGTON MANOR

de Mohun – Luttrell – Malet

The Manor House at Poyntington, formerly a property of the de Mohun family and their Luttrell successors at Dunster Castle, became the seat of the Malet family. Sir Thomas Malet (died 1665), a justice of the King's Bench, lost his son Baldwin in an impetuous Royalist ambush of Parliamentary forces passing through the deep-cut valley at the end of the Civil War, in 1646. Dame Joan Malet inherited the estate when Sir Thomas died. It then passed to their son Sir John Malet but the next Baldwin Malet, his son and heir, moved to West Quantoxhead, near Taunton.

Tenant farmers followed. Poyntington, historically, is a Somerset parish, being one of the three north of Sherborne that were transferred to Dorset in 1896.

PUNCKNOWLE MANOR

Napier

Stone harmony with the Napier family home at 'Punnel' being a model of perfection

The neat and perfect stone-roofed house beside the churchyard wall at Punnel – as Puncknowle is known – was the home of the Napier family for three centuries. They arrived from Scotland, after a short interlude behind the western end of the Chesil Beach at Swyre, with James and Hillary Napier who were in residence at Punnel in Tudor times. Their third son, the

judge Sir Robert Napier (died 1615), was Chief Baron of the Exchequer in Ireland, subsequently the Member of Parliament for Bridport, in 1601, and then Wareham, from 1603. His philanthropic gift to the county was Napper's Mite, the attractive almshouses built in Portland stone in South Street, Dorchester.

Sir Nathaniel Napier inherited Punnel Manor and the family's second home, Middlemarsh Hall between Minterne Magna and Hermitage, but then moved to Crichel House.

His sons were Sir Gerard Napier, who stayed at Crichel, and Robert Napier (1611–86), who returned to Punnel and became auditor of the Duchy of Cornwall and Receiver-General for financing Royalist forces during the Civil War. His leading opponent, Sir Thomas Fairfax, shielded him from any severe penalty, and the office was renewed after the Restoration, in 1663. His first wife was Anne Corrance and their son, Sir Robert Napier (1642–1700) was High Sheriff of Dorset and MP for Weymouth and then Dorchester.

Another branch of the family moved to Baglake at Long Bredy.

PURSE CAUNDLE MANOR

Aleyn — Lang — Hanham — Hoskyns –- Mews — Herbert — Barnes

John Aleyn, who held the manor until his death in 1293, was a Serjeant of the Forest of Blackmore whose tasks included 'tending and lodging the King's sick or injured dogs for his Lord the King's keeping when his Lord the King courses wild beasts.' He was also responsible for maintaining the pale around the medieval deer park at Gillingham. Roger Aleyn, born in 1269, succeeded his father. In the reign of Henry VI the Aleyn male line died out and Purse Caundle, with 575 acres, passed to Richard Lang in 1429 for 100 marks of silver.

The fifteenth-century manor house at Purse Caundle, sandwiched in Dorset's northern hills between the Somerset parishes of Milborne Port and Henstridge, was built by the Long family, as their name became spelt. Next were their cousins in the Hanham family, Richard Hanham and son William, in 1528. They lost Purse Caundle in the Civil War but a junior branch of the Hanham family remained in Dorset for the rest of the millennium, having settled at Dean's Court in Wimborne. John Hoskyns bought the property from Cromwell's Commonwealth Commissioners.

Meanwhile, having been born at Purse Caundle in 1619, Peter Mews progressed from war to religion. Having fought for the King at the Battle of Naseby he rose through the hierarchy of the Church of England, becoming Bishop of Bath and Wells, and then Bishop of Winchester from 1684 to 1706. Following the Hoskyns were the Huddleston family for nearly 150 years. Lady Victoria Herbert (1874–1957), daughter of the Earl of Carnarvon, made Purse Caundle her home from the turn of the twentieth century. Oliver Barnes then bought it.

RACEDOWN

Pinney — Wordsworth

Standing above the 500-feet contour in the hills between Birdsmoor Gate and Blackdown the Georgian house at Racedown had only two storeys when built by John Frederick Pinney of Bettiscombe in 1758. The third storey was added by John Pretor Pinney in 1790, for his father-in-law, and he coined the name Racedown. The square box-like shape was constructed from variegated bricks which were fired in an adjoining field.

Its claim to fame came between 1795 and 1797 when John Pretor Pinney's son, another John Frederick Pinney, lent Racedown to the poet William Wordsworth and his sister Dorothy. William wrote *The Borderers* here and they entertained Samuel Taylor Coleridge, visiting from Nether Stowey, during their final summer in west Dorset. He persuaded the Wordsworths to return with him to the Quantock Hills.

Major-General Sir Reginald Pinney extended the house. His military career extended from Victorian India to South Africa in the Boer War, Edwardian Egypt, and through the Great War in the trenches. He commanded the 35th Division and then the 33rd Division, in France and Belgium, from 1916 to 1919. He died in 1943 and his widow, Lady Hester Pinney, lived at Racedown until her death in 1958. Their eldest son was killed in Libya in 1941.

The Pinney family residence at Racedown, home of poet William Wordsworth and sister Dorothy, seen in the snow of February 1976

RANSTON

de Bruyn — Ryves — Baker — Littlehales Baker

The country house in parkland on the south side of Shroton village is contemporary with the centuries-old Shroton Fair which was held here for half a millennium, on 25 and 26 September, for horses, cattle and cheese. A medieval tithing, owned by the de Bruyn family, Ranston was bought and gentrified by Robert Ryves of Blandford in 1545. His descendants sold the house to Peter William Baker in 1781.

Baker was the agent of the London end of the Portman estate, in Marylebone, where he left his name in the most famous fictional address in world literature. He is the Baker of Baker Street (ask any Sherlock Holmes fan). His cousin, Sir Edward Littlehales, inherited the estate and adopted the Baker name, in 1814.

A century later it was the home of Lieutenant-Colonel Sir Randolf Littlehales Baker (1879–1959), Member of Parliament for North Dorset from 1910 to 1918, who was twice wounded in the Great War. Nicholas Baker (born 1923) returned to the family seat in the House of Commons in 1979.

REMPSTONE HALL

Rose — Calcraft — Marston — Ryder

The Rempstone estate between Corfe Castle and Poole Harbour was purchased from the Rose family in 1757 by libertarian politician John Calcraft (1726–72) who proceeded to buy most of the houses in Wareham. He was the illegitimate son of Henry Fox, 1st Lord Holland, under whose patronage he became Deputy Paymaster for the Army raised by the Duke of Cumberland in 1745. From 1768 he was Member of Parliament for Rochester and was credited with 'the best head for intrigue' among William Pitt's followers. He had his heart set on an earldom, coveting the title Earl of Ormonde, but died before it could be achieved.

Calcraft fathered six children by two mistresses, Mrs George Anne Bellamy and Miss Bride, both highly fashionable actresses. His eldest legitimate son, John Calcraft (1765–1831) was elected Member of Parliament for Wareham, at the age of twenty in July 1786, by virtue of the fact that his father had bought most of the town. He took the Rochester seat after his father's death but returned to Wareham for his final poll. This was followed by his political suicide, literally, resulting from the reproaches of his Tory friends. Calcraft had reverted to his old Whig principles and was the single changed-mind vote that carried the Reform Bill on 22 March 1831.

John Calcraft's death, on a Sunday morning in September 1831 'threw all Dorsetshire into combustion,' Mary Frampton wrote. 'He had never been happy since his reception in London, after he had been returned for Dorsetshire. A gloomy melancholy never left him, and he put a period to his existence by cutting his throat, and was found by his daughter, on her return from church, quite dead in this horrid manner. His eldest son, married to the Duke of Manchester's daughter, was residing at Rempstone, the family place, and the first notice of the event was the express which was sent to acquaint him with the catastrophe; and instantly the first inquiry made was, who would offer themselves to represent the county?' The candidates would be William Ponsonby and Lord Ashley, with the latter being elected, with a majority of 36 votes in the riotous poll which took place in ancient Poundbury Camp at Dorchester.

Captain John Hales Montagu Calcraft, the heir to the estate, also went into politics but died suddenly at Rempstone Hall after winning the Wareham Parliamentary seat by 13 votes in November 1868. Lady Caroline Calcraft and William Montagu Calcraft were in residence at the end of the century. By the time of the Great War it was the home of Commander Guy Montagu Marston.

The Ryder family have been in residence since. Major Dudley Claud Douglas Ryder transformed the scenery by striking a deal with the Forestry Commission to cover Rempstone Heath with conifers. Then came oil exploration and the discovery of Britain's biggest on-shore oilfield, at Wytch Farm in 1971, which has been developed by British Petroleum.

ROUND CHIMNEYS FARM

Churchill − Marlborough

The first Sir Winston Churchill (1620–1688) was born at Round Chimneys Farm near Glanvilles Wootton. A cavalier, who forfeited his estates after the Civil War, he was a Member of Parliament, fellow of the newly-formed Royal Society, and member of the Board of Green Cloth in the royal household. They advised the Lord Steward with resolutions such as this on 12 June 1681; 'Order was this day given that the Maids of Honour should have cherry-tarts instead of gooseberry-tarts, it being observed that cherries are threepence a pound.'

Sir Winston wrote a history of English Kings, *Divi Britannici*, and looked forward to Fridays. We know that from a letter to John Gibbon who documented the Fatality of Days: 'I have made great experience of the truth of it; and have set down Friday as my own lucky day; the day on which I was born, christened, married and, I believe, will be the day of my death. The day whereon I have had sundry deliverances – too long to relate – from peril by sea and land, perils by false brethren, perils of law suits, &c. I was knighted, by chance unexpected by myself, on the same day. And am so superstitious in the belief of its good omen that I chose to begin any considerable action that concerns me on the same day.'

Sir Winston was eclipsed by his famous son, John Churchill, 1st Duke of Marlborough (1650–1722), born at Round Chimneys Farm, who was known as Corporal John. His advancement was helped by the fact that his sister, Arabella Churchill (1648–1730) was mistress of the Duke of York, later King James II. Having saved the life of the Duke of Monmouth at Maastricht in 1673 he ended it in 1685, as second in command of the troops that suppressed the Western Rebellion.

As 1st Baron Churchill of Sandridge he defected, however, with 5000 men to Prince of Orange in 1688. He fought in Ireland and the Netherlands and was sent back by Queen Anne as Commander in Chief of the Allied Armies of England and Holland in the War of Spanish Succession. Brilliant actions at

The arms of Churchill, once of these parts, with its great names having re-entered Dorset family history at Canford and Minterne

Kaiserswerth, Venloi and Liege drove the French out of Spanish Gelderland in 1702. He was created Duke of Marlborough and crowned his military and social career with a bloody victory at the Battle of Blenheim in 1704.

He changed the history of Europe by preventing the French from joining the Bavarians. For this he was rewarded by a grateful nation, with the manor of Woodstock, Oxfordshire, and the building of Blenheim Palace. It was said of him that, as with Alexander the Great, 'he never lost a battle nor failed a siege'. Later successes were offset by intrigues at home and an imperious Duchess of Marlborough, confidant of Queen Anne and Keeper of the Privy Purse. The former Miss Sarah Jennings (1660–1744) tactlessly alienated the Queen though she left a fortune.

The eldest daughter, Lady Anne Churchill, married Charles Spencer, 3rd Earl of Sunderland (1674–1722) in 1700. The Marlborough dukedom passed to Charles Spencer, 3rd Duke of Marlborough and 5th Earl of Sunderland (1706–58) on the death of his maternal aunt who was Duchess of Marlborough in her own right. Round Chimneys Farm therefore has its place in the roots of two of England's most famous families with other connections at Minterne Magna where the Churchills also owned land and Canford Manor which has its links with the latter-day Sir Winston.

Round Chimneys Farm, at Glanvilles Wootton, was the birthplace of John Churchill

John Churchill, 1st Duke of Marlborough, presented with Blenheim Palace by a grateful nation

RUSHMORE HOUSE

Pitt — Rivers — Pitt-Rivers

Dorset has its Hardy Country in the Frome valley but the chalk downs of Cranborne Chase, straddling the Wiltshire borderlands, will forever be Pitt-Rivers Country. Here the Victorian father of archaeology, turned

Arms of the house of Pitt, which progresses through our story from Encombe and Kingston Maurward to an unlikely heir on the uplands of Cranborne Chase

Lieutenant-General Augustus Pitt-Rivers who turned archaeology into a science

'The General' as an enduring Roman presence

digging into a science, excavating and recording ancient civilisations while developing the Larmer Grounds as the first theme park and establishing a Gypsy School at Farnham. The latter became the Pitt-Rivers Museum when one failed social experiment was replaced by another. There is still a Pitt-Rivers Museum, in Oxford, but the Dorset collection of comparative ethnology – explaining cultural evolution as a global common cause – was closed and dispersed in the 1960s. Most of the General's laudable ideas and ideals were half a century ahead of their time. The last was cremation, at the only crematorium in the land which was in Woking, though he failed to convince his wife. 'Damn it woman, you shall burn!' he said, but she survived him and is buried beside the urn in Tollard Royal parish church.

Lieutenant-General Augustus Henry Lane Fox Pitt-Rivers (1827–1900) of the Grenadier Guards fulfilled a destiny that came through providence in a reverse form to the way that fate unfolds in Hardy's Wessex novels. His progress towards Rushmore estate, its 31,000 acres of Wiltshire and Dorset was through a succession just as unlikely as that in *Kind Hearts and Coronets*. The General was born Augustus Henry Lane Fox at Hope Hall, Yorkshire on 14 April 1827. He was the son of William Augustus Lane Fox and Lady Caroline Douglas, daughter of John Douglas, 18th Earl of Morton. He experimented with rifle ballistics and fought in the Crimea at Alma and Sebastopol. In 1853 he married the Honourable Alice Margaret Stanley, daughter of the 2nd Baron Stanley of Alderley and Henrietta Dennis, daughter of the 13th Viscount Dillon.

Then Major-General, he assumed the name Pitt-Rivers by royal licence in 1880 on eventually inheriting the property left by his great-uncle, George Pitt, 2nd Baron Rivers (1751–1828). He often told the story of how he visited the Rivers property before the Crimean War and realised it was studded with prehistoric remains. He mused how desirable it would be for an antiquary to inherit the estate but almost immediately dismissed the notion as an impossibility. There were twelve lines between him and the succession. Then 'a strange series of accidents and incidents' befell them. Even after the funerals of the 3rd Baron and the 4th Baron adverse odds seemed insurmountable. Conveniently, however, the 5th Baron Rivers sired eight daughters but no son. Horace Pitt, 6th Baron Rivers, obligingly remained childless and died in 1880.

The General took up residence in Rushmore House. A vice-president of the Society of Antiquaries and president of the Anthropological Institute he became the first inspector of ancient monuments on the passing of the Ancient Monuments Protection Act, in 1882. Still on the active list he was promoted Lieutenant-General the same year.

Thomas Hardy visited outdoor performances on the temple stage in the Larmer Grounds and was captivated by the General's daughter, writing a poem *For Agnes*. Agnes Lane Pitt, Lady Grove (1864–1926) started her *Who's Who* entry with the words 'voteless and unrepresented'. Though she had married Sir Walter Grove in 1882, and had four children, she was a thoroughly modern woman. Her globe-trotting included a crossing of the Atlas Mountains to meet Sultan Abdul-Aziz. At home she became president of the Forward Suffrage Union and addressed a series of lively public meetings. Once she was 'lying stark naked on a chaise-longue at Rushmore,' Michael Pitt-Rivers recounted, when his grandmother, Ruth Pitt-Rivers, entered the room. Agnes told her, 'You are now looking at the body of the most beautiful woman in the world.'

The estate passed to Captain George Henry Lane Fox Pitt-Rivers (1890–1966) who lived in its western offshoot at the Manor House, Hinton St Mary. Here he put a new gloss on many of the General's interests, turning anthropology into 'ethnogenics' with papers on race and population. Then came the Second

World War and internment in Brixton from 1940 to 1942 under Defence Regulation 18b for membership of the British Union of Fascists. He put this in his *Who's Who* entry as 'held a political prisoner by order of the Home Secretary'. A final chance to contribute to archaeological debate came with the discovery of one of the most important Roman mosaics ever found, in his home village of Hinton St Mary. Now in the British Museum, and described as a depiction of Christ, Captain Pitt-Rivers published a contrary opinion and convincingly argued that in fact it depicts the Emperor Constantine. His third and last marriage was to Stella Edith Howson Clive.

Open-air theatre in the 1890s, in the Larmer Tree Grounds, created by General Pitt-Rivers between Farnham and Tollard Royal

The family home at Tollard Royal became King John's House where his heir Michael Pitt-Rivers managed an estate that was reduced to its core 7500 acres of historic hills and parkland. He took a particular pride in its heritage status and revived Cranborne Chase Conservation Society. For decades an atheist he told me his childhood ambition was 'to be a Prince Bishop of the Church'. He went on, in the words of foreign correspondent Michael Davidson, to seek 'philosophical goodness in such systems of thought and experience as Buddhism.' When their friend Edward Montagu of Beaulieu was 'charged with a certain offence' Pitt-Rivers joined Davidson and Robin Maugham in a quiet campaign behind the scenes that succeeded a decade later in liberalising the law against homosexual activities.

Michael Pitt-Rivers married Sonia Orwell, the widow of George Orwell. Sandroyd School, from Chobham, was evacuated to Rushmore House in the Second World War. The General had introduced golf to its grounds – of 60 acres of idyllic inner park inside a further 400 acres of outer parkland – and Michael Pitt-Rivers re-established a nine-hole golf course.

Rushmore House, at the heart of the immense estate inherited against the odds by General Pitt-Rivers

Famous names galore have passed through Sandroyd, at Chobham and Rushmore, where Andrew Brisbane showed me portraits in the school library. Randolph Churchill, son of Winston, took a Dorset bride from Minterne House. Anthony Eden from East Knoyle became Prime Minister (and gave us Suez). Michael Ramsey became the 100th Archbishop of Canterbury when Geoffrey Fisher retired to Trent. Sir Max Aitken was a hero of the Battle of Britain. Sir Charles Madden represented the Royal Navy. Sir Terence Rattigan wrote plays. Tony Armstrong-Jones married Princess Margaret. Tim Sainsbury

Temple and cricket pavilion in the grounds at Rushmore

became Britain's top grocer. Nick Pocock captained Hampshire cricket. Sir Ranulph Fiennes grows icicles in his beard. Peter Carrington became Defence Minister and went to NATO (though the Crichel Down scandal nearly destroyed his political career before it started). Ian Gow MP was blown up by the IRA. The prince who would have been King of Yugoslavia was eliminated by Tito.

The school had forgotten the fate of His Majesty King Faisal II of Iraq and invited him to a Rushmore speech day. 'Maybe it would be advisable to speak to your history master,' the school secretary was told. (The King had been assassinated some twenty-five years earlier.) Another invitation was sent to the classy-sounding Morton Hall in Lincolnshire. 'It is possible we have one or more Sandroydians here,' the school was told. 'I must reluctantly inform you that they are unlikely to be available.' (Morton Hall is one of Her Majesty's Prisons.)

Michael Pitt-Rivers, the General's grandson, in his study at King John's House

SADBOROW

Bragge — Eyre

Together with Forde Abbey, the Bragge family house on the hill in Thorncombe parish came to Dorset from Devon, in a boundary change of 1844. It was designed by Leicester architect John Johnson who made his name in London and was the County Surveyor for Essex. William Bragge employed him in 1773 to rebuild Sadborow around a domed staircase. Grounds of 50 acres surround the hilltop.

Captain John Arthur Bragge was the descendant in residence a century later, and through the Great War, followed by an empty period in the 1930s. It is now the home of the Eyre family. George Eyre was a land agent for Somerset County Council.

SAINT GILES HOUSE

Malmayne — Plecy — Hamely — Ashley — Cooper —
Ashley-Cooper — Shaftesbury

The Dorset family with the longest attachment to a single seat and the greatest catalogue of all-round fame has held the same land for what is set to be a millennium. The manorial estate around St Giles House, we are told, has not changed hands by purchase since the Norman Conquest. The descent was from the Malmayne family, via an heiress, to the Plecy family. Their male line died out and the heiress was married to Sir James Hamely (died 1398). They had no children and the estate went to Sir John's daughter by his second marriage. She married Robert Ashley, from across the border in Wiltshire, and they and the Ashley Coopers (both with and without a hyphen) have been in residence since 1400.

Its present great house, built by the Cooper family in Renaissance style in 1650, replaced the Ashley family's modest manor house of a century earlier, and spans both family names which became aristocratic in the aftermath of the upheavals of Civil War and the republican experiment. The first among the foremost was a politician who had inherited these lands at the age of ten and went on to fight with the Parliamentary Army, leading it in the storming of Abbotsbury and bringing relief to beleaguered Taunton, and becoming a competent post-war administrator for the Commonwealth regime. Then he spanned the divide between Cromwell and the Restoration as one of the twelve emissaries who went to Holland in May 1660, to negotiate terms for the return of King Charles II. He was created Baron Ashley in 1661 and was Chancellor of the Exchequer for the next eleven years.

The 'Shaftesbury Papers' of Anthony Ashley Cooper, 1st Baron Ashley and 1st Earl of Shaftesbury (1622–83), show the extent to which he had one of the greatest philosophers of the age acting as his servant, secretary, speech adviser, and prompter. John Locke (1632–1704) became his master's voice in 1672, the year Ashley was created Earl of Shaftesbury in April and was then, in November, appointed Lord Chancellor of England. He founded the Whig Party.

Anthony Ashley Cooper, 1st Earl of Shaftesbury and Lord High Chancellor of England, in 1672

Much of their joint work, however, passed through Shaftesbury's London residence, Exeter House, and other offices in the capital. They shared intellectual stimulation, as is shown by the list of books Shaftesbury took back with him to St Giles House, in parkland beside the road into Cranborne from Wimborne, in 1774. From these, in 1690, Locke found the source material which became milestones in the development of libertarian dogma-free thought, in *An Essay Concerning Humane Understanding* and *Two Treatises of Civil Government*.

The originator of the Admiralty charts, with which the British would, to quote Tennyson, 'sail wherever a ship may sail, and found many a mighty state', was Sir Anthony Ashley (1551–1628) of St Giles House. He has a magnificent tomb in Wimborne St Giles parish church. As Clerk of the Privy Council, he had been shown the first known collection of maritime charts, which were produced in Holland in 1584, and his English versions came out in the Armada year of 1588, replete with tributes to Charles Howard, 2nd Baron Howard of Effingham, for his achievements in smashing the Spanish fleet, and not forgetting Sir Francis Drake for his pre-emptive attack on Cadiz: The sub-title of *The Mariners Mirror of Navigation*, here in modernised English, sets out its scope:

> First made and set forth in diverse exact Sea Charts by that famous navigator Luke Wagenar of Enchusien, and now fitted with necessary additions for the use of Englishmen by Anthony Ashley. Herein also may be understood the exploits lately achieved by the Right Honourable Lord Admiral of Her Majesty's Navy, and some former services does by that worthy knight Sir Francis Drake.

The memorial to Anthony Ashley Cooper in Wimborne St Giles parish church

'A celebrated author' say the largest words, in capitals, on the memorial to Anthony Ashley Cooper, 3rd Earl of Shaftesbury (1671–1713) in Wimborne St Giles parish church. He had the philosopher John Locke as his tutor and featured as the 'shapeless lump' in John Dryden's satire on the first earl. Anthony Ashley Cooper, then Lord Ashley, was elected to Parliament for Poole in 1695 and made his maiden speech in support of prisoners at treason trials being allowed representation by lawyers. He fluffed his words but brilliantly capitalised upon the error: 'If I am so confounded by a first speech that I cannot express my thoughts, what must be the condition of a man pleading for his life without assistance!'

He wrote a study on ethics entitled an *Inquiry concerning Virtue* in which he coined the phrase 'moral sense'. This had considerable influence among European writers generally but, says *The Dictionary of National Biography*, his style – 'always laboured, often bombastic' – led to inevitable neglect of his writings, to the extent that his 'former vogue has become scarcely intelligible'.

Moral outrage was left to a descendant to articulate. The lasting fame of the family from St Giles House is safe in the shape of a neat and handsome Christian aristocrat whose mind was fixed upon the tortured lives and landscapes that are usually unimaginable in the deep-green Tory splendour of inherited wealth and privilege. Antony Ashley Cooper, 7th Earl of Shaftesbury (1801–85) took on the mantle of his father's estate and title in 1851. He had entered Parliament as Lord Ashley in 1825, as the member for Woodstock, and set to work reforming the Lunacy Acts. From 1830 to 1846 he sat in the House of Commons for Dorchester and then the Dorset county constituency.

Anthony Ashley Cooper, 7th Earl of Shaftesbury, Victorian 'friend of the friendless'

He threw his considerable energies into what became the most successful one-man philanthropic crusade in English history. Yet this was not single-issue fanaticism; his was an obsessive force for good on a wide range of fronts.

He expanded the Factory Acts into new industries and removed numerous abuses of women and children in the mines. Boys as young as four were being harnessed in chains and used for shifts of up to 18 hours shuffling on all fours as they dragged trucks along coal seams. By 1842 he secured the ban on women of any age and boys under thirteen years of age being employed underground.

The scandal of the 'climbing boys' was then remedied – preventing the use of small children as human chimney-sweeps – and from 1847, now sitting for Bath, Lord Ashley championed the education of Midland and northern slum children in the Ragged Schools. Shaftesbury, as he became on entering the House of Lords after his father's death, put the amelioration of social wrongs above party politics and indeed had no conception of the sea-change he was causing in working-class expectations and power. Though he never saw it as such, he had blurred the divisions between rich and poor, and in restoring some dignity and hope in the latter he defused the chances of a revolution in England, which might have come to pass during what was only the 'Red

St Giles House, about 1800, the seat of the Earls of Shaftesbury

Mirage' of 1919. Lower-class aspirations were met by the Victorians by democratic change with legislation conceded on their behalf by the ruling classes. Worker power was therefore set to find its twentieth-century expression inside rather than outside the political system.

Shaftesbury created the new England for a Labour Party rather than its Marxist alternative. Eight years after his death, a memorial was unveiled in London's Piccadilly Circus on 29 June 1893 to the 7th Earl. That it is what we know as Eros did not escape contemporary censure. For, years before, a committee had commissioned Alfred Gilbert (1854–1934) – who was knighted in 1932 – to produce something more appropriate to perpetuate the Earl's memory as the nation's greatest philanthropist. Gilbert had been recommended by Auguste Rodin as being 'a hundred worlds better than Benvenuto Cellini'.

The gentlemen of the committee had expected a full-length statue of Lord Shaftesbury but Gilbert visualised something more symbolic and without clothes, there being, he insisted, 'no need for gratification of a tailor'. What transpired was a representation not of a naked Lord Shaftesbury but a lithe Eros, the Greek god of love, soaring on tiptoe and firing his shaft into the crowd. He is set above a fountain bursting with the waters of charity which issue forth from the mouths of fish and crustaceans.

In this context of Modern Art the intention of including a bust of the Earl was abandoned as inappropriate. Gilbert also outspent his budget twice over, and this prevented him from 'completing the design with eight basins of irregular shape, such as Bernini would have designed had he the delicacy and refined taste'.

Eros did not immediately win the hearts of Londoners. Initially they called him Cupid and the joke was coined that he was 'burying shafts'. *The Times* dismissed it as 'the ugliest monument'. From the start it was destined to be known as Eros, at once the most famous of London monuments, rather than the 'Shaftesbury Memorial' as was envisaged. Artistically it is its own justification – but the contemporary resentment has to be seen in the light of how twentieth-century society would have reacted, say, to a Henry Moore statue of Sir Winston Churchill immortalising his electioneering quip, 'Madam, all babies look like me.'

Lord Shaftesbury's grandson, the long-lived Anthony Ashley-Cooper, 9th Earl of Shaftesbury (1869–1961), was Provincial Grand Master of Dorsetshire from 1902 to 1952 and Chairman of Dorset County Council from 1924 until 1946. He also presided over numerous charities and boards, from the Shaftesbury Society and English Church Union, and was Lord Steward of His Majesty's Household from 1922 till George V's death in 1936. Across the water, before partition, he was Lord Mayor of Belfast in 1907, and Chancellor of Queen's University till 1923. A cavalry-man, he had joined the 10th Hussars in 1890, and commanded the North Irish Horse from 1902 to 1912, returning home for the Great War, as Brigadier-General commanding the 1st South-West Mounted Brigade from 1913 to 1916, when he was also Lord Chamberlain to Queen Mary, until 1922.

He outlived his son and heir, Major Lord Ashley, and the title passed to the latter's only son, Anthony Ashley-Cooper, 10th Earl of Shaftesbury (born 1938), who chaired the council of the London Philharmonic Orchestra and is an honorary American citizen of South Carolina.

SANDFORD ORCAS MANOR

Knoyle — Hutchings — Medlycott

Historically belonging to Somerset, until transfer to Dorset in boundary changes of 1896, the Tudor mansion at Sandford Orcas dates from a complete rebuilding of a much older house within a year or two of 1535, when it was in the ownership of the Knoyle family. The Manor House, in golden Hamstone, encloses a courtyard, with a matching gatehouse projecting towards the parish church. For a compelling combination of architecture and setting, it is arguably the most sublime house in either county; Somerset's loss was definitely Dorset's gain.

The non-geographical element of the Sandford Orcas name derives in a corrupted state from de Orescuiltz owners of Norman times. The Knoyles arrived in about 1400. By the end of the century, from 1492, William Knoyle was Sheriff of both Somerset and Dorset.

Edward Knoyle, who rebuilt the house, married Catherine Martyn from Athelhampton. The same master mason worked on both houses. The Knoyles remained in residence at Sandford Orcas until 1732. They were followed by the Hutchings family who then rented it to tenant farmers. Hubert Hutchings bequeathed the property to a cousin, Sir Hubert Medlycott, of Ven House at Milborne Port, in 1880. Ven remained their main seat for another nine decades, until the death of Sir Christopher Medlycott, after which his son, Sir Mervyn Medlycott, returned to Sandford Orcas.

Jerrards, a sub-division of the manor of Sandford Orcas, which was split in 1480, takes its name from the Gerard family. The house is from that date but was enlarged in 1616 which is the date accompanying the arms of Gerard carved in the porch.

Sandford Orcas Manor, the seat of the Medlycott family, in 1963

SHERBORNE CASTLE

le Poure — Raleigh — Digby — Bristol — Wingfield-Digby

Sir Walter Raleigh, Queen Elizabeth's favourite mariner, was given the Old Castle at Sherborne

Sir Walter Raleigh, with his son, in 1602

Built as a hunting lodge, across 'moorish ground' from what is now Old Sherborne Castle, the replacement Sherborne Castle was given its country-house role by Sir Walter Raleigh (1552–1618). Initially, in 1592, Queen Elizabeth's favourite mariner took over the Old Castle. The latter had been built by Bishop Roger le Poure, the founder of Salisbury Cathedral, early in the twelfth century. Raleigh attempted repairs and inserted windows but tired of the persistent mould and in 1594 abandoned the attempt at converting the existing castle into a home worthy of his style and status.

The new Sherborne Lodge arose with four towers and Dutch-style curves around the top of the facade. Dressed stone came from Ham Hill and rubble from the curtain wall of the Old Castle. The latter looked rough and the innovative solution was plastering. It is one of the earliest plastered houses in the land. It was also ahead of its time in having big leaded-light windows, taking up a large proportion of the available wall space, though many were reduced or removed during later expansion of the house. After the Old Castle was reduced to a ruin, for holding out against the Parliamentary Army during the Civil War, the rebuilt Sherborne Lodge became known as Sherborne Castle.

The Digby family were brought to Dorset by diplomat and statesman Sir John Digby, 1st Earl of Bristol (1580–1653), from Coleshill, Warwickshire, after Sir Walter Raleigh lost Sherborne Castle and then his home and his head. Digby also had his period of disfavour and imprisonment in the Tower of London. The son of Sir George Digby and Abigail Henningham – the daughter of Sir Arthur Henningham – he married Beatrix Dyve, the widow of Sir John Dyve and daughter of Charles Walcot.

Their son George Digby, 2nd Earl of Bristol (1612–76), born in Madrid during his father's ambassadorship there, had a Spanish boyhood and returned to England to petition the House of Commons at the age of twelve for the release of his father from the Tower. His complex personality was summed up by Horace Walpole: 'A singular person whose life was one contradiction. He wrote against poetry and embraced it; he was a zealous opponent of the Court and a sacrifice for it; was conscientiously converted in the midst of his prosecution of Lord Strafford and was most unconscientiously a persecutor of Lord Clarendon. With great parts he always hurt himself and his friends; with romantic bravery he was always an unsuccessful commander. He spoke for the Test Act though a Roman Catholic, and addicted himself to astrology on the birthday of true philosophy.'

Having sat for Dorset in the 'Short' and 'Long' Parliaments he changed sides during the Civil War and commanded 400 Royalist horsemen at the Battle of Edgehill on 23 October 1642. It was the first major fight of the conflict. Digby impetuously failed to hold back his force in reserve but in the event they were not needed as Colonel Charles Essex and the Parliamentary Army fell back to Warwick and London. That left King Charles free to secure Oxford.

George Digby displayed conspicuous gallantry in the taking of Lichfield into which he rode like a steeplechaser and was shot through the thigh. He then fell out with his commander, the King's nephew Prince Rupert, and joined the Court at Oxford where he succeeded Lord Falkland as Secretary of State and conducted affairs in a manner described as 'both unfortunate and imprudent'. On 16 October 1645 he was back in the field, taking over from Prince Rupert as

Lieutenant-General of the King's Northern Forces. Defeated by Sir John Brown at Carlisle Sands he fled with Sir Marmaduke Langdale to Scotland, the Isle of Man, Ireland, the Scilly Isles, Jersey and France. He eventually volunteered for the French king's war of the Fronde, showing great gallantry, and became a Lieutenant General of the French army in 1651, in command of royal troops in Normandy. Sir George Digby, nominated a Knight of the Garter by the exiled King in January 1653, succeeded his father as Earl of Bristol the same month. His military career progressed to Austria, with a diplomatic diversion on a secret mission to meet the Spanish king in Madrid, before the Restoration of King Charles II enabled him to return to London's political stage.

George Digby married Lady Anne Russell, the second daughter of Francis Russell, 4th Earl of Bedford. Their eldest son, John Digby, 3rd Earl of Bristol (died 1698), married Alice Bourne, the daughter of Robert Bourne, and then Rachel Wyndham, the daughter of Sir Hubert Wyndham. Two rich heiresses brought him resources but there were no children from either marriage and the earldom of Bristol died with him.

The other Digby family title dated back to the son of Sir Robert Digby and Lettice, Baroness Offaly. Robert Digby, 1st Baron Digby of Geashill (died 1642), had the barony created for him in 1620. His first marriage was to Sarah Boyle, the daughter of Richard Boyle, 1st Earl of Cork, and the widow of Sir Thomas Moore. Their son was Kildare Digby, 2nd Baron Digby (died 1661) who married Mary Gardiner, the son of Londoner Robert Gardiner. This prolific branch of the family lived in Coleshill and three of their sons took the title in succession – Robert Digby, 3rd Baron Digby (1654–77), Simon Digby, 4th Baron Digby (1657–85) and William Digby, 5th Baron Digby (1660–1752).

William Digby took the title more than half way through the next century. Known as 'Good Lord Digby', he married Jane Noel, daughter of Edward Noel, 1st Earl of Gainsborough, and outlived their sons John (died 1747) and Robert (died 1726). The latter, a Parliamentarian, has a literary monument in Sherborne Abbey, with the eulogy being by family friend and poet Alexander Pope (1688–1744) who is commemorated by Alexander Pope's Seat across the cascade from Raleigh's Seat in Sherborne Park. He also provided the poetical inscription, in Sherborne Abbey, for Mary Digby who was the eldest sister of John and Robert Digby.

The title skipped a generation and passed to William's grandson, Edward Digby, 6th Baron Digby (1730–57) who was the son of Edward Digby and

The Old Castle, abandoned by Raleigh and stormed in the Civil War, as a romantic ruin in 1857

Sherborne Lodge, as it was engraved by George Cooke, became known as Sherborne Castle

Charlotte Fox, the daughter of Sir Stephen Fox. In 1756 the 6th Baron, a dapper aesthete who appreciated art and nature, commissioned Lancelot 'Capability' Brown to change the landscape between the two Sherborne castles, by making cascades and transforming the Yeo stream into a vast sheet of water. As a philanthropist, disguised each time in the same shabby blue coat, he would visit London each Christmas in order to bribe or buy the freedom of prisoners, taking 30 at a time 'to the George Inn in the Borough where a dinner was ordered for the happy wretches he was about to liberate.' Potentially one of the most interesting members of the family, his demise occurred during a visit to an estate he owned in Ireland, after a combination of excess alcohol and the effects of the common cold, which progressed to pneumonia and put him into a fatal fever.

Sherborne Castle, its south front, in 1857

Half-created, the eastern side of the enhancement project across Sherborne Park was brought to completion by his brother, Henry Digby, 7th Baron Digby and 1st Earl Digby (1731–93). He built the graceful and classical triple-arched Pinford Bridge, designed by Robert Mylne, in 1790. The peerage of Earl Digby in the county of Lincoln and Viscount Coleshill in the county of Warwick was created in November 1790 'as head of a noble and worthy family'. His brother, Canon William Digby, was Dean of Durham Cathedral.

Henry Digby's second marriage was to Mary Knowler, the daughter of John Knowler, but their son Edward Digby, 8th Baron Digby and 2nd Earl Digby (1773–1856) never married. The short-lived Digby earldom died with him but the double baronies of Digby, in the English and Irish titles, passed to his first cousin once removed, Edward St Vincent Digby, who has already been mentioned under Minterne House.

Sherborne Castle was inherited by the offspring of Edward Digby's sister, Charlotte Maria Digby, who had married William Wingfield-Baker. It was now the home of the Wingfield-Digby family. Through the past two centuries they have represented the full gambit of applied gentrification, from the Army and Blackmore Vale Foxhounds through to Parliament, the Church, and the national arts collections. The following three generations were fairly representative.

The arms of the Wingfield-Digby branch of the family

John Kenelm Digby Wingfield-Digby MP (1859–1904) represented North Dorset and had a number of sons.

Rev. Stephen Harold Wingfield-Digby (1872–1942), chaplain to the 4th Car Division in France in the Great War, came home to be vicar of Sherborne Abbey from 1916 to 1932, and semi-retired to the Kiamber chaplaincy in Kenya Colony. Colonel Frederick James Bosworth Digby Wingfield-Digby (1885–1952), Master of the Blackmore Vale Hunt from 1909, served with the Dorset Yeomanry from 1915 to 1918, in the Middle East campaigns from Gallipoli to Egypt, Palestine and Syria. Major Kenelm Essex Wingfield-Digby (born 1891) served in the Royal Horse and Royal Field Artillery, in France in the first half of the Great War, and then in Mesopotamia, going on to Ireland for the Troubles from 1919 to 1923.

Simon Wingfield-Digby MP (1910–2000), eldest son of Colonel F.J.B. Wingfield-Digby, served in the campaign from Normandy to the Baltic and represented West Dorset from 1941 to 1974. His brother, George Frederick Wingfield-Digby (1911–89), the Keeper Emeritus of the Victoria and Albert Museum, was a world expert in tapestries, embroidery and Islamic carpets and textiles.

George Wingfield-Digby, Master of the Blackmore Vale Hunt, 1858–65, provided Sherborne with the Digby Assembly Rooms and hosted lavish social events

SMEDMORE HOUSE

Clavell — Richards — Mansel

A single enduring family name has been attached to grey shale cliffs around Kimmeridge Bay from before the reign of Richard II. It became a nationally known one with Sir William Clavell, an industrial entrepreneur making alum and glass, and nephew John Clavell (1603–42), a gentleman poet and robber. His volume entitled *A recantation of an ill-led Life; or a Discoverie of the Highway Law*, in verse, saved his neck from a sentence of death in 1627.

Clavell is even on the map, with Clavell's Hard – long ago inaccessible and unusable – and the precariously-placed Clavell Tower seamark. Although it was built by the Rev. John Richards, in 1830, he adopted the Clavell name on inheriting the Smedmore estate, from William Richards who moved from Warmwell House in 1806.

The unbroken lineage found a fresh link with its ancient roots when the estate passed by marriage to the Mansel family. Major Rhys Mansel, through a sequence of memorials and parish records across the Isle of Purbeck, claimed descent from Walter de Clavile who arrived after the Norman Conquest.

His best known tenant was the historian Sir Arthur Bryant but the family is back in residence and set to enter its second millennium there.

Gentleman poet and highwayman John Clavell (1603–42) was the nephew of Sir Willaim Clavell of Kimmeridge

SOUTH LYTCHETT HOUSE

Jeffrey – Lees

Built as Sans Souci – 'No worries' – by John Jeffrey MP, South Lytchett House stands in the parkland of a 3500-acre estate, to the north of the main road between Lytchett Minster and Upton. It became the home of Sir Claude Scott in about 1810. By the end of the century, already re-named, it was the home of Sir Elliott Lees (1860–1908). Member of Parliament for Oldham, and then Birkenhead, he was a director of the *People* newspaper, being created baronet in 1897.

Sans Souci, as South Lytchett House was known, having 'No worries' for John Jeffrey in 1796

Accomplished on horseback, he was Master of the South Dorset Hunt, and won the House of Commons Point to Point three times. He took command of

the 26th Dorsetshire Company of the Imperial Yeomanry for the Boer War, in 1900, and returned from South Africa with the Distinguished Service Order and five clasps.

Sir Elliott Lees married Florence Keith in 1882. Their eldest son, Sir Thomas Evans Keith Lees (1886–1915), inherited the title but was killed on the Western Front. His brother, Captain Sir John Victor Elliott Lees (1887–1955), succeeded as the third baronet, and was severely wounded in Flanders during the Great War.

In 1915 Captain Lees married Madeline Pelly, the daughter of Sir Harold Pelly of Thorngrove, Gillingham. Between the wars he commanded the 4th Battalion, the Dorsetshire Regiment, and its 5th (Territorial) Battalion on the outbreak of the next war in 1939. Sir John and Lady Lees lost their elder son, Captain James Lees, in action in 1945. The family home was transferred to the smaller mansion of Post Green, across the road, and the title passed to their second son, Thomas Edward Lees.

SOE officer and Serbophile Michael Lees (1921–92)

A grandson of Sir Elliott Lees, born at Lytchett Minster, the outstanding hero of this military family was Michael Lees (1921–92). He was parachuted into Yugoslavia in June 1943 as leader of a Special Operations Executive mission to liaise with Chetnik guerrillas. They fell into land held by a Bulgarian unit and many of Lees's men were butchered as they lay wounded. He managed to re-group and persuaded General Mihailovic to blow up two strategic sections of railway and six German trains.

Then the Allies changed allegiance, from Mihailovic's Serbs to Tito's Partisans, and Michael Lees spent the rest of his life researching the volte-face that imposed communism on Yugoslavia for forty-five years as a direct result of British duplicity. He documented the case that Winston Churchill had been bamboozled by one-sided information. Mihailovic and his men remained loyal to their King and the Allies but were crushed by Tito and executed as traitors. Lees was withdrawn to Italy, where he met and married a FANY (First Aid Nursing Yeomanry) officer, Gwen Johnson.

He was then parachuted back into action, to escort two delegates from the Piedmontese liberation committee over the Maritime Alps, wiping out a German artillery post in order to reach the American lines. His third mission, with Major Roy Farren of the SAS, was to attack German headquarters in a villa in Albania, in the course of which Lees collapsed down the stairwell with four bullets inside him. He was smuggled to safety in the bottom of an ox-drawn manure cart, followed by a flight to hospital in Naples, in a spotter-plane from a mountain terrace.

Wartime Maquis, politician and journalist Dodo Lees (1920–91)

Michael Lees published the secret story of Mihailovic's downfall in 1990 and was feted in Yugoslavia where he predicted that the Serbs would again lose out – through international media and political partiality – to the Croats. Despite declining health he mounted a one-man campaign from Krajina enclave to the Westminster lobbies and addressed a series of public meetings in Canada.

His obituary writer in *The Times* concluded: 'Lees spent the day he died at his desk intent on his crusade. He had brought to it the great force of personality, the single-mindedness and the courage which had characterised his life. It is not given to many men to die happy in fighting a cause first embraced in youth.'

The family also had its heroine who shared Hitler's birthday, 20 April, and was told by him that it meant she would be an accomplished public speaker. Dodo

Lees, later Mrs Delores Selby Bennett (1920–91), took advantage of her family connection with Sir Alan Brooke, Chief of the Imperial General Staff, to wangle a Red Cross assignment with the French Maquis behind German lines. She was awarded the Croix de Guerre and bar for dragging out wounded men under fire and through minefields. Post-war she was personal staff officer to Marshal Leclerc, the charismatic Frenchman who had accepted the surrender of Paris, in August 1944. He was killed in November 1947, in an air crash in Algeria, when he was about to take command of French Indo-China.

Back in Dorset, to the dismay of the family, she became a prospective Parliamentary candidate for the Labour Party, and fought Brendan Bracken in Bournemouth East. That was hardly a credible challenge, in 1949, but she went on almost to unseat her cousin, Fitzroy Maclean, at Lancaster in 1951. She could have moved on to a safe seat but chose instead to follow her future husband, Commander 'Chipps' Selby Bennett, to Malta where she became private adviser to colonial leader Dom Mintoff.

Returning to Dorset, in 1962, she was credited with a decisive role in helping Guy Barnett to capture the South Dorset seat for Labour. Finally, in a characteristic double twist of family and party allegiances, she unsuccessfully stood against her husband when he sought election as a Conservative to Dorset County Council. Then she clashed with fellow members of the Labour Party by urging them to reconsider moves to ban fox-hunting.

STALBRIDGE PARK

Boyle — Cork

Robert Boyle (1627–91) of Stalbridge Park gave us Boyle's Law

The first complete classical house in Dorset stood in Stalbridge Park behind a thick drystone wall that encloses the land between the village and the county boundary with Somerset. Designed by Isaac de Caus, who worked with Inigo Jones on Wilton House, it was demolished after fire damage, in 1822, but the roadside entrance retains superb seventeenth-century stone gate-piers surmounted with stone lions.

These were the emblem of Richard Boyle, 1st Earl of Cork (1566–1643) who bought Stalbridge Park and planned the rebuilding of its house in 1638. His youngest 'seventh son and fourteenth child' was the chemist Robert Boyle (1637–1691) of 'Boyle's Law' fame who came to live at Stalbridge as a child but was in Geneva with a brother when their father and eldest brother were killed during the rebellion in Ireland. They heard the news on returning to England, in Civil War turmoil, the following year. Robert Boyle had inherited Stalbridge but the chaos was such that it took him another four months to get there.

His lasting fame rests on his scientific work but a lighter look at life, inspired by holidays at Stalbridge, appears in his *Occasional Reflections upon Several Subjects* which was published in 1665. It inspired Jonathan Swift's satirical *Occasional Meditations on a Broomstick*. Boyle died in London, at the house of a sister who had died only a week before on Christmas Eve in 1691. They are buried at St Martin's-in-the-Fields, beside Trafalgar Square.

Boyle's lions still watch over the entrance to Stalbridge Park

STEPLETON HOUSE

The grand house in Stalbridge Park was destroyed by fire

de Stepleton — Daccomb — Pitt — Fownes — Beckford —
Pitt-Rivers — Lindsay — Robinson

The de Stepleton name survives as that of a grand house in the otherwise almost unpopulated parish of Iwerne Stepleton. They were followed by the Daccomb family from whom the manor passed to Sir William Pitt of Stratfieldsaye in about 1610. Then came the coincidence of two owners who shared an obsession.

Fox-hunting in England has its physical and philosophical roots at Stepleton House between the chalk escarpment and the River Stour to the north of Blandford. Thomas Fownes established kennels for a pack of hounds and asserted his claim to ancient sporting rights by taking them up Smugglers' Lane into Cranborne Chase.

In 1745 he sold the house and 90-acre park to Julines Beckford, son of the Honourable Peter Beckford, Governor and Commander-in-Chief of Jamaica. The house was still unfinished in 1762 when Edward Gibbon dined with Beckford and found it 'unmeaning, expensive and unfinished'. The prognosis of the decline and fall of Stepleton House was greatly exaggerated, however, as not only does 1763 appear as the date on a replacement window but its great age was about to dawn.

Huntsman Peter Beckford, of Stepleton House, painted in 1779

The son of Julines Beckford, Peter Beckford (1740–1811), had taken to the saddle and the chase, and went on to share his hunting expertise with the wider world by publishing his *Thoughts upon Hare and Fox Hunting; also an account of the most celebrated Dog Kennels in the Kingdom*. It is the first book to describe hunting methodology. In the author's account of *Dorset Sporting Runs* mention is made of its Stepleton pedigree — quoting a hairy crossing of the nearby river — but he stands corrected as to where it was written.

Stepleton House in 1857

Beckford at the time, in 1781, was recovering from being thrown from his horse and had written most of the book while incapacitated at Hotwells health spa in the Avon Gorge at Bristol. He also jotted down more abstract aspects of the subject, from scent and hound-breeding to how the Greeks hunted, in *Essays on Hunting*. His command of languages was legendary; 'He would bag a fox in Greek, find a hare in Latin, inspect his kennels in Italian, and direct the economy of his stables in exquisite French.'

In 1773 he married Louisa Pitt, daughter of George Pitt, 1st Baron Rivers (1722–1803), and they obtained a special patent in 1802 for their son, William Horace Beckford, to succeed to the barony on the death of the next and unmarried George Pitt, 2nd Baron Rivers (1751–1828). In taking the title, when his uncle died, William Horace Beckford, 3rd Baron Rivers of Sudeley Castle, changed his family name to Pitt-Rivers.

Stepleton remained with the family into the twentieth century, when the Honourable Miss Pitt rented it to the Honourable Ronald Charles Lindsay (1877–1945), fifth son of the 26th Earl of Crawford and Balcarres. Having become the Right Honourable Sir Ronald Lindsay, British Ambassador in Constantinople, he bought the house. His career proceeded, as our man in Berlin, and then to Washington. He was the British Ambassador to the United

The frontage of Stepleton House unchanged in 1948

States for the whole of the 1930s. He retired to Dorset as the world went to war and lived to see final victory, over Japan, a couple of weeks before his death on 21 August 1945.

His first wife, Martha Cameron from Pennsylvania, died in 1918. Lindsay married again in 1924. Elizabeth Sherman was the daughter of Colgate Hoyt of New York. Stepleton was inherited by Lindsay's nephew, the Earl of Crawford, and became the home of Mrs Stanley Robinson.

SYDLING COURT

Hardye — Sidney — Smith — Marriott — North —
Guilford — Miskin — Millar — Aldred

Medieval in origin, held by the Hardye family and Elizabethan poet and soldier Sir Philip Sidney (1554–86), not that he lived there, the Court House stands beside the churchyard at Sydling St Nicholas. It was bought by Sir William Smith MP in 1718 and remained the home of Smiths for a century and a half. They had it stucco-faced circa 1790. Sir William Smith, knight, was Sheriff of Dorset, Sheriff of Middlesex and Alderman of London. Sir John Smith, the first Sydling baronet, was Sheriff of Dorset in 1773. Sir John Wyldbore Smith, second baronet, also held the post. Then Sir John James Smith broke with the City connections and went native as Colonel of the Dorset Militia.

Their family vault, inserted beneath the chancel of the parish church, is walled with lavish Georgian statuary, dating from 1745 'where the bodies of so many of our kindred are laid in the sure and certain hope of the Resurrection'.

Sir William Marriott had the Gothic frontage of Court House built in the 1860s. Each May the Court Leet still met there. Dudley Francis North, 7th Earl Guilford (1851–85), moved to Sydling Court on taking over the Cattistock Hunt in 1882. He was also President of the Dorchester Agricultural Society. A dashing young horseman, he always led the field from the front, and came to grief in a 'rasper' of a hedge near Castle Hill, Duntish, on 19 December 1885. He died that evening, of a ruptured liver, on being brought home to Sydling.

The arms of Smith

Sydling Court, in 1815, the seat of Sir John Smith

Sydling Court and St Nicholas parish church in 1857

His body was taken by train, from Maiden Newton, to the family seat at Waldershare Castle, Kent. Lord Guilford's title was inherited by his son, Frederick, at the age of nine.

Indian veteran Major William Lancelot Miskin MC (1887–1950) retired to Sydling Court and organised the village Home Guard in 1940. Meanwhile, George Millar (born 1910) was going through the conflict with exploits which rivalled those of Sir Philip Sidney. He was a former *Daily Telegraph* and *Express* reporter who went on to make news. Having escaped from an Italian prisoner of war camp he returned to Britain and then to the war by being parachuted into France as a secret agent to organise the French Resistance. Post-war, he wrote up his biography, and farmed a thousand acres of the valley and its downs from Sydling Court.

The arms of Smith, plus pineapple, adorn the gates. Current occupants are Diane and Gavin Aldred.

THORNHILL HOUSE

Thornhill — Boucher — Parke — Wynne-Jones

The greatest monument to Dorset man Sir James Thornhill (1675–1734), the son of Walter Thornhill from Wareham and Mary Sydenham of Wynford Eagle, is even more impressive than the Last Supper painting in St Mary's Church in his home town of Weymouth. It is instead a national treasure, the Painted Hall at the Royal Hospital, Greenwich, which is now the officers' mess of the Royal Naval College. This took him more than twenty years to complete and is on such a huge scale that even at a knock-down rate of £1 per square yard – he had requested £5 – Thornhill's eventual fees totalled £6,685. 2s. 4d.

He started in 1707 and by the time he finished he was rich and famous, having been appointed Sergeant-Painter to the King in 1720; the first painter to be knighted, in 1721; and Member of Parliament for the Weymouth seat of Melcombe Regis from 1722 to 1734.

His moneys enabled him to acquire the lost family seat at Thornhill Park in the Blackmore Vale, on the hill between Stalbridge and Lydlinch, where he built a classical house and an obelisk, commemorating George I's accession to the throne. At Blenheim his opulent ceiling shows another Dorset man, John Churchill, 1st Duke of Marlborough, ex-Round Chimneys Farm at Glanvilles Wootton, in his finest hour. He is depicted at his moment of victory in the Battle of Blenheim which made him the national hero and earned him Blenheim Palace as his thank you.

In monochrome (reduced rate, £2 per square yard), Thornhill painted the inside of the cupola at St Paul's Cathedral. In Dorset his country-house work includes a ceiling at Charborough Park. Sir James Thornhill's only daughter was the wife of a notable painter of a very different kind in the next generation. She eloped with William Hogarth.

Thornhill House was bought by William Boucher (died 1836) who left £500 for the relief of the poor 'being members of the Church of England' in the tithing of Thornhill. The conditions and schedule of investments, including £200 in Stalbridge Gas Company, are set out on a huge board in the porch of Stalbridge parish church.

Crimean veteran General Sir William Parke (1822–97), who retired to Thornhill House, became aide-de-camp to Queen Victoria, from 1859 to 1872. He was Colonel of the Seaforth Highlanders and went from the war in the Black Sea to the campaigns in central India.

Refurbishment of the house took place in 1927 and it was acquired by Major Charles Llewelyn Wynne-Jones (1890–1974) of the Somerset Yeomanry who lost two of his sons in the Second World War.

TOLLER FRATRUM

Samways – Fulford – Wynford

'Toller of the Brothers' in the valley west of Maiden Newton is named for the Brethren of St John of Jerusalem, generally known as the Knights Hospitalers, whose connection with the manor was through its ownership by the Abbess of Buckland, Somerset. The nuns of Buckland Priory pledged obedience to the Brethren of St John. John Samways of Martinstown bought Toller Whelme after the Dissolution of the Monasteries, in 1540, and rebuilt the house.

John Samways (died 1586) was succeeded by Robert Samways (died 1621) whose younger brother inherited the property. Bernard Samways (died 1645)

Little Toller Farm at Toller Fratrum where the refectory of the Knights of St John of Jerusalem is thought to have been in the thatched barn (right)

reached the age of ninety-six. The property then passed by marriage from the Samways family to the Fulfords who gave their name to Great Fulford, Devon, and adopted these west Dorset hills for more than a century.

Now known as Little Toller Farm, it came into the ownership of Lord Wynford of Wynford Eagle, in 1867.

TRENT MANOR

Storke — Gerard — Wyndham — King Charles II — Seymour — Hohler

The most famous short-term resident of Trent was William Jackson. Mr Jackson was also known as His Majesty King Charles II. The nation's runaway monarch, fleeing for his life from defeat at the Battle of Worcester, spent a total of nineteen days at the house, in its hiding place above the kitchen beneath floorboards in Lady Wyndham's chamber. He departed but was forced to return after an abortive attempt to board a boat at Charmouth. His second and successful departure was via Heale House, near Salisbury, to Shoreham and exile in France.

Previous occupants of Trent Manor, also in troubled times, were the Storke and Gerard families. The latter, as Catholics, had constructed the refuge to hide the occasional harassed priest. Mary Storke married William Gerard, from Jerrards

Charles I, disguised as a lady, on the next leg of his escape after hiding in Trent Manor

at Sandford Orcas, in the reign of Henry VIII. Their notable scholar was Thomas Gerard (1595–1634) who wrote *A Survey of Dorsetshire* – the county's first book – though when it was eventually published, in London in 1732, it carried the name of John Coker of Mappowder. The Wyndham family came to Trent when Anne Gerard, the second daughter of Thomas the antiquary, married Colonel Francis Wyndham.

As with nearby Sandford Orcas and Poyntington, Trent was transferred from Somerset to Dorset, in 1896. By this time and for the next half century Trent Manor was owned by Miss Jane Seymour, who inherited it as a young girl on the death of her father, Alfred Seymour. It became the home of Gerald and Margaret Hohler.

Trent Manor in 1930

TYNEHAM HOUSE

Russell — Chyke — Pope — Williams — Lawrence — Bond

The surviving medieval hall of Tyneham House dates from about 1350 when the coastal valley between Lulworth and Kimmeridge was owned by a branch of the Russell family whose name still attaches to the Dorset landscape from Kingston Russell in the west to Russel (sic) Quay on Poole Harbour in the east. Tyneham then passed via the Russell female line to the Chyke family and then John Pope who sold it to John Williams of Winterborne Herringston in 1523. Though often wrongly described, in status it was a country house rather than a manor house, as Tyneham had no manor.

The Elizabethan main wing of Tyneham House and its new north porch, built in 1861, with Thomas Bond (brother of owner Prebendary John Bond) beside the east entrance

The first extensions to the hall were carried out by John Williams's younger son, Henry Williams, between 1567 and 1583. In the seventeenth century, after the Civil War, Tyneham passed to Sir Robert Lawrence of Creech Grange when he married heiress Jane Williams. Their son, John Lawrence, sold it to Nathaniel Bond in 1683 and then proceeded to part with Creech Grange as well. It became the Bond family tradition for senior members of the family to live in the Grange and for younger sons to move over the hill to Tyneham. The Elizabethan extensions to the house were rebuilt by Rev. William Bond in 1820 who made the main rooms loftier and more spacious and added the north porch. Rev. John Bond and the antiquary Thomas Bond shared its idyllic setting in Victorian times.

William Henry Bond followed, and married Mary Meysey Thompson, the sister of Lord Knaresborough. Their son, Ralph Garneys Bond (1880–1952) entered the Sudan Political Service and was Governor of Dongola and Fung provinces. In retirement, while commanding the Tyneham platoon of the wartime Home Guard, he was fated to be the last private owner of Tyneham, when the entire parish was requisitioned by Southern Command to more than double the size of the Lulworth tank firing ranges on 19 December 1943.

UDDENS HOUSE

Harris — Greathed — de Pentheny-O'Kelly

Ruins of the north-east gable of Tyneham House, in 1972, after removal of the north porch

One of the lost country houses of Dorset, Uddens was the home John Greathed Harris, of the Middle Temple, who was Deputy-Judge Advocate on the continent of Europe from 1815 until his retirement in 1819. His grandson, Major-General William Wilberforce Harris Greathed (1826–78) was a lucky hero. A soldier of Empire, as a youth he was the first officer to force his way through the breach that ended the siege of Mooltan in the second Sikh War, on 2 January 1849. Whilst working as a consultant railway engineer at Allahabad he heard of the mutiny at Meerut and the rebel seizure of Delhi in May 1857.

Orders came from John Russell Colvin, Lieutenant-Governor of the North-West Provinces, for Greathed to carry despatches and command a company of English volunteer cavalry. He became the first traveller from 'Down Country' to ride the gauntlet into Meerut and later, taking messages from Colvin to Lord Canning, he was the last European to find a way between Alygurh and Meerut for four months. He led the attack of the Delhi Field Force in the battle to take the ridge at Badlee-ka-Serai on 8 June 1857.

The day nearly ended differently, when a small group of Britons found themselves surrounded by Pandees. Greathed drew his sword and led a rush that turned into a successful break-out as the enemy fled. He was severely wounded, however, in the assault on Delhi. By the new year he had recovered sufficiently to act as the Royal Engineer directing the crucial attack that broke the long siege of rebel-held Lucknow.

British power restored, Greathed consolidated its grip by building more railways. He invaded China with Sir Robert Napier in 1860 and was in the vanguard of the campaign up to the capture of Peking, at which point he returned to England with despatches. His last military task was in home waters, building 'Palmerston Follies', as Prime Minister Viscount Palmerston's super but superfluous fortifications became known. He directed operations on the colossal defences around the naval harbour of Plymouth in 1867, moving on to the Bristol Channel, where a line of fortifications was constructed from Brean Down, via the islands of Steep Holm and Flat Holm, to Lavernock Point in Wales.

Uddens House, in a 50-acre park, was the residence of Lieutenant-Colonel Edgar J. de Pentheny-O'Kelly, until dereliction after the Second World War. It was then demolished and the site is now surrounded by dense pine plantations between Ferndown and Holt.

UPCERNE MANOR HOUSE

Raleigh — Mellor — White — Batten — Mount Batten — Broadhead

Having passed from the Sherborne lands of the Bishop of Salisbury, via Sir Walter Raleigh, the downland bowl at the head of the Cerne valley was acquired by Sir Robert Mellor (died 1624) of Winterborne Came. Upcerne Manor House, completed 1601, incorporates stonework from the ruins of Cerne Abbey. The White and Batten families followed.

Colonel John Mount Batten (1843–1916) was in residence at the turn of the twentieth century. He was High Sheriff of Dorset in 1903 and then Lord Lieutenant for the county. His son, Captain John Henry Strode Batten, was killed in the Great War. The property was inherited by the Colonel's daughter, Winifred Eleanor Sarah Batten. Wilfrid Street was in residence in the Second World War.

The shape of the landscape was changed by Reginald and Vera Broadhead who demolished redundant thatched cottages and created a picturesque lake below the Manor House. They also took over the parish church – 'to use as a private chapel' – in 1971.

The idyllic setting of Upcerne Manor, between parkland and the escarpment at the head of the Cerne valley, in 2002

UPTON HOUSE

Seymour – Tichborne – Doughty – Llewellin

In parkland beside Holes Bay at the northern extremity of Poole Harbour, Upton House was the home of Henry Seymour (1776–1849), High Sheriff of Dorset in 1835. His illegitimate daughter found herself at the centre of a Victorian national sensation. Born in France, Henriette Felicite Seymour (died 1868) married Sir John Francis Tichborne (1784–1862), who succeeded his brother Sir Edward Tichborne Doughty (1782–1853). Sir John was the tenth baronet and his eldest son and heir was Roger Charles Doughty Tichborne (born 1829).

What happened to Roger gave rise to the great Tichborne Trial in 1873. Arthur Orton, the son of a Wapping butcher, an identification made by the jury on the balance of probability rather than any proof, was convicted of impersonating Sir Roger Tichborne who had been given up for drowned – en route to Jamaica – in 1854 and legally declared dead. Orton, a bush-ranger from Australia, was able to convince Roger's mother that he was her son, and likewise the family doctor and solicitor, old servants and those who had gone punt-gunning with him in the harbour as a boy. He was also able to cast flies into the Test as well as any native gentry. The *Poole Pilot* newspaper championed the case of the Tichborne Claimant.

Upton House, near Poole, featured in a sensational Victorian trial

A phalanx of other witnesses, also including members of the family, were adamant that he was not Roger. Many had a financial interest in the matter. The title had gone to his brother, Sir Alfred Joseph Tichborne, the eleventh baronet who died before his son and heir was born, Sir Henry Alfred Joseph Tichborne (1866–1910), the twelfth baronet.

Facing the music: the Tichborne Galop

Roger was brought to Upton House for the funeral of his uncle, Sir Henry Joseph Tichborne (1779–1845), the eighth baronet. Sir Edward Doughty wanted to sell Upton but young Roger fought the plans, preferring the maritime location of the Doughty home at Upton to Tichborne Park at Cheriton, on the Hampshire Downs. The family did not make Tichborne their home until 1848.

Roger refused to go there, said he intended leaving the Army to go travelling, and was offered Upton House. Lady Doughty wrote to him: 'We earnestly hope you may be comfortable at Upton, and I shall always cherish a hope the day may come when you are a settled and happy man.' Roger had to finish his military service, at Canterbury, and make three visits to Paris, and his last outing in the Dorset countryside was riding to hounds in December 1852.

John Moore, the son of the Upton butler, went with Roger Tichborne to Le Havre where they sailed on 1 March 1853 in the French sailing ship *La Pauline*, for Valparaiso. Here they received the news that Sir Edward Doughty had died, with the title passing to Roger's father, and Roger now the heir to the Tichborne lands and fortune. John Moore was left in Santiago, having been taken ill, and Roger went on to Peru, crossed the Andes to Buenos Aires and went on to Rio. Here he drank heavily and took arsenic to counter 'spasms of the heart' which had him 'raving and foaming at the mouth like a mad dog'. He sailed on the *Bella*, with a cargo of coffee, for Jamaica and New York. They left Rio on 20 April 1854 and were never heard of again, though wreckage of a ship's boat from the *Bella* was seen off the coast of Brazil four days later.

The Tichborne family let Upton for the remainder of the century. It was sold to William Llewellin in 1900. He married Frances Mary Wigan and their son, Colonel John Jestyn Llewellin, 1st Baron Llewellin (1893–1957) commanded the Dorset Heavy Brigade. Then, as MP for Uxbridge from 1929 to 1945, he held several Government posts concluding with Minister of Food from 1943 until the Labour landslide. His final posting was to the colonies as Governor-General of the Federation of Rhodesia and Nyasaland from 1953.

Lord Llewellin never married and the title died with him. Upton House was acquired by Poole Borough Council and the grounds took on a new lease of life as Upton Country Park. The house is the venue for conferences and events.

Baffling pose of the Tichborne Claimant as a contemporary porcelain figure

WADDON HOUSE

Gerard — Reymes — Chafin — Vye — Corbett — Chaffyn-Grove

Once important and large, Waddon House faces the Fleet hinterland from a hillside at Portesham, and retains a graceful west wing of Queen Anne style above stone gate-piers and walnut trees, chosen for Farmer Boldwood's home by the film-makers of *Far from the Madding Crowd*. It was the manor of East Waddon or Gerard's Waddon, owned by Thomas Gerard of Trent Manor, who compiled the *Survey of Dorsetshire* in the 1620s. His heirs were three daughters and the eldest married Colonel Bullen Reymes who fought for King Charles in the Civil War and was rewarded with appointment as Vice-Admiral of Dorset at the Restoration. He was Member of Parliament for Melcombe Regis and undertook a diplomatic mission in Tangier. Reymes's son left a widow who married Harry Chafin from Zeals in Wiltshire. They expanded the house, with the addition of the surviving wing, but fire then destroyed the older parts in 1704.

Waddon House became a rustic farmhouse, with dairyman Job Vine in residence in late-Victorian times. It was gentrified by B.O. Corbett after his arrival in 1928, and the Chafin name has since returned, with Charles Chaffyn-Grove currently in residence.

Waddon House, near Portesham, is the home of farmer William Boldwood in the cinema version of Thomas Hardy's Far from the Madding Crowd

WARMWELL HOUSE

Trenchard — Sadler — Richards — Foster — Best — Wynford — Law — Ellenborough — Ross-Skinner

One of the many seats of the Trenchards, following acquisition by Sir Thomas Trenchard of Wolfeton in 1526, Warmwell House became the home in 1662 of the Hebrew and Arabic scholar John Sadler (1615–74). He married Jane Trenchard in 1645 and received £10,000 of her father's fortune. The master of Magdalene College, Cambridge, from 1650 till the Restoration, Sadler was the pivotal figure in the Court of Chancery who enabled the Jews to build a synagogue in London. He was given to premonitions and credited with two notable predictions. During a bout of illness at Warmwell in 1662 he made the prophecy to the rector, Rev. Cuthbert Bound, that London would experience a Great Plague, and that it would be followed by the Great Fire, in which 'the greatest part of the city would be burnt, and St Paul's Cathedral.'

The destruction of 1666 included his own London home. Then his mansion in his home county of Shropshire went up in flames. Dispossessions followed, as the penalty for serving Oliver Cromwell, and deprived him of all his other properties except Warmwell, where Jane lived with their 14 children.

By the end of the century, John Richards was in residence at Warmwell House, and became known as 'the Pepys of south Dorset'. His diary, now in Dorset Record Office, was transcribed for the author by his descendant Arthur Richards, the auctioneer in Sturminster Newton. It shows a character so bigoted that it is worthy of a satirist.

He enjoyed a wager as only a true gentleman can. On 24 July 1679: 'Mr Penny layd me 2 bottles of claret that Barcelona was taken by the French, and this day in their possession, and 6 bottles more that the Duke of Saxony remained not King of Poland.' By the time the news seeped through to Dorset, Penny won his two bottles, but Richards had the best of the bet as the Duke still ruled Poland.

Squire Richards was not universally liked, as this entry for 9 August 1697 confirms: 'At a County Court held this day in Dorchester, my brother James and I were nominated for coroners, but it being opposed by Mr Byles, Mr Gillingham &c, the election fell on Mr Arnold and Mr Gerard Wood'.

On 10 October 1697 Thomas Symes 'came hither to borrow £20 of me, but he went away without it'. Squire Richards falls out with everyone, from Hunibon the shepherd to his wife Alice, from whom he keep himself 'strange'. After a couple of days, on Friday 23 February 1700, she gives him an ultimatum that he must mend his manners: 'Upon which insolence, losing all patience I burnt my will before her eyes.'

On Monday morning, Alice Richards sets off at 05.00 hours for Puddletown, 'to meet ye Dorchester coach for London'. She does not seem to have stayed there

Warmwell House, from the south in a Frome valley landscape, in 1857

long for on 21 July 'qta notte dormivo in cellar chamber pesser in riposta dal ecla' which roughly translated is: 'This night I slept in the cellar to be at rest from her.'

As might be expected, he drank hard and suffered gout, particularly in June 1699: 'Last night the gout came into my left foot, and all this day it was very troublesome, but much worse on Tuesday the 27th. About noon this day I applyd 5 leaches to it, next day ye 28, was very severe and all that night much worse not permitting a moment's sleep.'

He seems to have been the victim of an elaborate practical joke on 29 December 1698: 'This afternoon about 4 o'clock came two Sherborne trumpeters to salute me as High Sheriff &c. An hour after 2 other from Captain Coker, on the same errand.' He came down to earth on 19 January 1699: 'Last Monday's *Gazette* which came by this day's post mentioned William Okedens being Sheriff for Dorset.'

A repeat performance by trumpeters on 7 January 1702 was followed by confirmation of his social demise: 'This afternoon I received the news of my being taken off from ye Shrievalty. Mr Hardy of Woolcomb, being put in my place.'

The Richards family stayed in residence at Warmwell until 1806 when William Richards inherited Smedmore House at Kimmeridge. The Foster family, notably Captain Augustus Foster who added the Victorian bay window, held it until the Great War when it became the home of Philip George Best, 6th Baron Wynford.

The next resident, Major Henry Astell Law, 7th Baron Ellenborough (1889–1945) more than reached the status that eluded John Richards. A Gentleman-at-Arms in His Majesty's Body Guard he held the Military Cross, from the Great War, and was Deputy-Lieutenant of Dorset.

He was followed by Colonel H. Crawley Ross-Skinner, and Harry J.C. Ross-Skinner, through the remainder of the twentieth century.

WATERSTON MANOR

Govis — Newburgh — Marney — Howard — Bindon — Suffolk — Strangways — Carter — Woodall — FitzGibbon — Tindall

Lower Waterston, between Puddletown and Piddlehinton, was the home of the Martyn family before their progress down the Piddle valley to Athelhampton Hall. By 1377 their male line at Waterston had died out and the property passed by marriage to the Govis family, Newburgh family, Marney family, and the 1st Lord Howard of Bindon. His younger son, Thomas Howard, received Waterston and rebuilt it in Elizabethan brick with plastered half-timbering above and a stone frontispiece, in 1586, before succeeding to Lulworth Castle, on his brother's death in 1590, as the 3rd Lord Howard of Bindon.

The Earl of Suffolk inherited the property in 1605 and sold it to Sir John Strangways in 1641, following which it remained one of the lesser homes on the immense estates of the Earls of Ilchester for more than 250 years, including a farmhouse interlude that has taken on a literary and legendary life all of its own.

The east front of Waterston Manor in 1816

South porch of Waterston Manor in 2002

That period of its existence ended in fire in 1863 though it was rebuilt in period style and then sold at the end of the century to Major-General Gerald Vernon Carter. Morley Horder carried out renovations for him in a scheme that restored the house, with its four acres of gardens and 28-acre grounds, as a country seat.

The house was immortalised by Thomas Hardy as Weatherbury, the inheritance of Bathsheba Everdene in *Far from the Madding Crowd*, though for the cinema film of the novel Bloxworth House was chosen as the setting. Lieutenant-Colonel Harold Whiteman Woodall (1872–1951), who bought Waterston in 1936, married Elizabeth Nora McLean and was Joint Master of the South Dorset Hunt.

The next owner, Robert Louise Constantine Lee-Dillon FitzGibbon (1919-83), was the author Constantine FitzGibbon. His many books included *Paradise Lost and More*, in 1959, and *Random Thoughts of a Fascist Hyena*, in 1963, followed by a biography of Dylan Thomas together with an edition of his letters. He then put Waterston on the market, at £35,000 in 1965, and returned to his Dublin roots. Works there took on nationalist themes, with *Red Hand*, *The Ulster Colony*, *The Life and Times of Eamon de Valera*, and a volume entitled *Drink*. Waterston Manor is now the home of the Tindall family.

WHATCOMBE HOUSE

Pleydell — Mansel-Pleydell — Pleydell-Railston

Edmund Morton Pleydell built Whatcombe House as 'a handsome commodious mansion' in 1710 to replace his former family seat in the village at Winterborne Whitechurch. The new home was set in 160 acres of well-wooded parkland immediately upstream from the village.

John Clavell Mansel-Pleydell (1817–1902), the elder son of Colonel John Mansel of Smedmore, set about publishing the first county-wide compilations of natural history records for Dorset. Whatcombe Herbarium contained the first

recorded specimen of Argentinean Spartina cord-grass which now covers thousands of acres of salt-marsh in Poole Harbour. He encouraged others to contribute to collections of flora and fauna and was elected president of the Dorset Natural History and Antiquarian Field Club, founded in 1877, which evolved into Dorset Natural History and Archaeological Society. Parishioners were provided with a Working Men's Club and Reading Room which was run for many years by Reginald James.

Mansel-Pleydell owned 9000 acres. In Whatcombe House he kept the natural sciences strongly represented on the shelves of one of the best libraries in Dorset. Walls were hung from floor to ceiling with 'a good collection of paintings by George Morland, Gainsborough, Zucchero, Van Dyke, Kneller, Lely, Jansen and Andrea del Sarto'.

His son, Lieutenant-Colonel Edmund Morton Mansel-Pleydell (died 1914), showed an interest in the natural history of the Indian sub-continent with recreations such as tiger-hunting and pig-sticking. Whatcombe House was inherited by Lieutenant-Colonel Henry George Morton Pleydell-Railston (1885–1936) who married Vivien Mansel-Pleydell. He was wounded in the Great War. Whatcombe now houses a Christian retreat managed by the Barnabas Fellowship.

WINTERBORNE CLENSTON

Herynge — de la Lynde — Morton — Pleydell — Tory

Behind a great six-bay barn of banded flint and stone, with a flourish of early-sixteenth-century style, the manor house at Winterborne Clenston has a circular porch which is unusual in being surmounted by a projecting gable rising from corbelled corners. The house, in the middle of the Winterborne valley of the central Dorset Downs, was the home of the de Winterborne family from 1230, whose topographical name derives from the nearby winter-flowing stream which becomes a carpet of grass in a normal summer. Their heiresses took the ownership through the Heryng and de la Lynde families.

The legend of the latter is that a 'beautiful and goodly white hart' was slain by one of their number, in the time of Henry III, beside King's Stag Bridge in the royal forest of the Blackmore Vale. He was a bailiff and the family then lived at Hartley. In punishment, an enraged Henry levied a tax known as White Hart Silver, and the de la Lyndes adopted three harts' heads as their arms. Sir Thomas de la Lynde, who died in 1532, carried out the Tudor renovations at Clenston.

The property passed to the Morton family of Milborne St Andrew and then the Pleydell family of Whatcombe. Harry Mansel-Pleydell rented the house to farmer William Rupert Tory in Edwardian times.

WOLFETON HOUSE

Mohun — Trenchard — Weston — Bankes — Zamoyska — Thimbleby

The confluence of the Cerne and Frome rivers, east of Charminster, is the setting for one of Dorset's most ancient houses. A moated Norman house was followed by a venerable eastern frontage which is now flanked by two round towers, with high slit windows, behind which the main building is 'more than usually distinguished by the size of its mullioned windows,' to quote Thomas Hardy on the Tudor insets. Its ancient owners were the Jourdains and Mohuns. The last of the latter, John Mohun (died 1480), was followed by the Trenchard family from Hordle, in the New Forest. At the heart of the Dorset Downs they found their forte as sheep farmers.

It was the Trenchard family who hosted an unexpected visit in January 1506 by Archduke Philip of Austria, his Spanish wife Joanna, and Princess Isabella of Aragon. Joanna's father was Ferdinand of Castile and they were en route there, from the Netherlands, to claim the throne. The party had taken refuge in Weymouth from a Channel gale and Sir Thomas Trenchard took the initiative of inviting them to Wolfeton.

The second chance event was even more remarkable. An invitation for an extended dinner led directly to the creation of the greatest ducal dynasty in British history giving the most unlikely of Dorset roots to one of the most powerful families in the land.

By chance Sir Thomas sent for his relation John Russell (1486–1555), from Berwick hamlet near Swyre, to act as interpreter. Russell, a well-travelled young man, had perfect Spanish and a compelling bonhomie. The visitors liked him and he was invaluable for conversation. Russell was therefore invited to accompany them to Windsor Castle, which started a sparkling life-long diplomatic career which saw him created Earl of Bedford. Having proved popular at Court he also had staying power and outlasted all other potential rivals. He gathered unbelievable wealth, including the royal forest and chase of Exmoor in 1539, and other land forfeited by Henry Courtenay, Marquis of Exeter; some 30 towns and manors which belonged to Tavistock Abbey; thousands of acres in Cambridgeshire from Thorney Abbey; the Cistercian Woburn Abbey, where he founded one of the nation's wealthiest ducal houses; and to cap it all, in 1552, seven acres of Convent Garden 'called Long Acre'.

Sir John Trenchard of Wolfeton as Principal Secretary of State to King William and Queen Mary

Wolfeton flourished and expanded with the Trenchards. It was frequently visited by King George III who expressed so much interest in the marble table in the drawing-room that it was presented to him and is now in the Royal Dairy at Frogmore, Windsor. The house fell on hard times with the departure of the Trenchards. Much was demolished, including ranges of buildings at each end, in the mid-nineteenth century. The family also removed their heraldic stained glass, showing linkage with numerous families and estates, and much was broken in the process of being carted to Lytchett Matravers.

Restoration followed at Wolfeton, including the addition of battlements admired by Thomas Hardy, after Dr W.H.P. Weston bought the property in 1862. He heightened the original south-east tower of the main house and built its matching north-east counterpart. In 1874 Wolfeton was bought by Wynne Alfred Bankes of Kingston Lacy. The Bankes family invited a Spanish princess, the Infanta Eulalia, to visit the house in 1901. Countess Zamoyska, a granddaughter of Wynne Bankes, inherited the house.

Wolfeton House is now owned by Nigel Thimbleby. It has a couple of well documented supernatural stories. The first is a gruesome premonition concerning the wife of Sir Thomas Trenchard. A visiting Assize Judge made his excuses and walked out on a dinner after having a vision of Lady Trenchard with her throat slit and her head under her arm. His carriage was called and was taking him back to Dorchester as Lady Trenchard committed suicide.

Another strange coincidence foretold the demise of King Charles I. Fourteen Kings of England are carved on the wainscot over the chimney. John Aubrey records that the figure of King Charles lost his sceptre, which fell from the figure while the family and a large party were dining in the parlour, on 3 November 1640. It was the day that the Long Parliament began to sit. The die was cast for the Civil War and a turbulent decade that culminated with Charles's execution.

WOODSFORD CASTLE

de Bryan — Fitzpaine — Butler — Ormonde — Stafford — Strangways — Ilchester

Remarkable for the biggest expanse of thatch on an inhabited building in the British Isles, Woodsford Castle is the perfect example of a fortified medieval manor house, having been licensed for crenellation by King Edward III in 1337. The rebuilding was carried out by William de Whitefield who granted the property to Sir Guy de Bryan, in 1368, and he leased it to Robert Fitzpaine in 1389.

On Sir Guy's death, in 1391, it descended down a female line to James Butler, Earl of Ormonde and Wiltshire, who met his end in the Wars of the Roses, on 29 March 1461. Though he survived the actual fighting, he fell in the merciless slaughter that followed in which Edward IV issued orders to take no prisoners, bringing the death toll among Henry VI's supporters to 37,000. The House of Lancaster had collapsed and the Yorkist victors rewarded Butler's cousin, Humphry Stafford of Hooke, with a knighthood as well as Butler's sequestered property. The Stafford name survives near Woodsford with the next village up the Frome valley being named West Stafford.

Sir Humphry Stafford unwisely changed his allegiance, to the Lancaster cause,

Victorian engravings of Woodsford Castle, by J.H. le Keux, dedicated to the owner, the Earl of Ilchester

and paid for his desertion with his life. Only three months after having been created Earl of Devon, in 1469, he was taken off and beheaded at Bridgwater in 1469. His cousin, Alainor Stafford, married Thomas Strangways, in whose family Woodsford would descend for the rest of the millennium, as part of the Earl of Ilchester's vast estates.

WOOLBRIDGE MANOR

Turberville — Howard — Weld

Thanks to Thomas Hardy, and its pivotal role as the setting for the tragic turn in *Tess of the d'Urbervilles*, Woolbridge Manor is known internationally as one of England's ancient family seats. Hardy tells us the story of the failing fortunes of the Turberville family whose main home at Bere Regis has long been a flat pasture called Court Green between the corner opposite the Royal Oak public house and the river.

Woolbridge Manor and the medieval bridge painted by H.J. Moule in 1886

The family had the chance to expand their estate southwards to Wool after Bindon Abbey, on the other side of the River Frome, lost its lands in the Dissolution of the Monasteries. Thomas Turberville grasped the opportunity but the dynasty that seemed so dynamic in the reigns of Henry VIII and Queen Elizabeth lost its male line in the reign of Queen Anne.

John Turberville (died 1623) married Lady Anne Howard of Lulworth Castle. The 'I.T. 1635' datestone on Woolbridge Manor is for their son, Sir John Turberville who was Sheriff of Dorset in 1652. He gave the building its char-

Woolbridge Manor as an hotel in 1965, living down the Tess experience

acterful chimneys but the equally distinctive gables are earlier, being contemporary with the humped Elizabethan bridge which gives the manor its name. Together they now make for one of the most photogenic settings in the county.

The last Thomas Turberville left twin daughters who were inseparable and lived together in a London house, in Fulham, where they reached the age of seventy-seven and died together on the same day. The Manor House at Bere Regis was demolished and that beside Woolbridge became a farmhouse. The southern lands of the Turbervilles went to the Weld family and the northern parts into Drax hands.

WRACKLEFORD HOUSE

Pope

The central figure in the development of the Dorchester Brewery was Alfred Pope of Clifton Maybank (1842–1934), the first chairman of Eldridge, Pope Limited, who built a town house at South Court in Dorchester and a country mansion at Wrackleford, near Stratton. His first wife was Mary Jenner Rolph, from Ontario, in 1869. She died in 1871. Their only son was Major Alfred Rolph Pope (1870–1951) of the 4th (Territorial) Battalion of the Dorsetshire Regiment. He lived in Culliford House at Dorchester.

Mrs Alfred Pope, the former Miss Elizabeth Mary Whiting, saw her sons troop off to war

His father's second marriage, in 1874, was to Elizabeth Mary Whiting from 'an old Kentish family settled in London'. Pope's second term as Mayor of Dorchester, in 1886, began by welcoming the Prince of Wales to the Bath and West of England Show. As well as hunting and shooting he carried out antiquarian research and published a study on *The Old Stone Crosses of Dorset*. In 1881 he was a member of the building committee of the new Dorset County Museum and gave to its library 'a superb set of the four volumes of the choice and rare second edition' of John Hutchins's county history. He acquired the Wrackleford estate in 1887 and built South Court in 1893.

One son, Sub-Lieutenant William Eldridge Pope (1881–1901) was in HMS *Hermione* in the Yangtze River when the Boxer Rebellion broke out in 1900 and European embassies in Peking were besieged. He led an attack from Hong Kong to quell native disturbances on the mainland. On returning from 'the salubrious climate of China' to 'bitter spring winds' in Portsmouth he was stricken with pneumonia and died in Haslar Hospital.

Alfred Pope (1842–1934) of Wrackleford House and the Dorchester Brewery

Alfred Pope had a total of 15 surviving children. All eleven of the boys served in the Great War, as did his three sons-in-law. Boer War veteran Lieutenant-Colonel Edward Alexander Pope (1875–1919), of the Welsh Regiment, lived at Woodbridge, Branksome Park, Poole. He was wounded in France in 1917 and suffered 'bronchial trouble, caused by mental strain and overwork', and succumbed to 'disease contracted on active service'.

Sergeant George Clement Pope (born 1876) served in the 1st Volunteer Battalion of the Dorsetshire Regiment and survived to fish for trout again in the Frome at Wrackleford.

Captain Charles Alfred Whiting Pope (1877–1917) was put in charge of a detachment of the Royal Army Medical Corps and sent to Egypt on the troopship *Transylvania* which was torpedoed in the Mediterranean on 4 May 1917.

He 'went down with the ship whilst dressing the wounds of the poor fellows who were hit by the explosion.' A total of 413 lost their lives.

Second-Lieutenant Percy Paris Pope (1882–1915) of the 1st Welsh Regiment was wounded and posted missing in a bayonet attack on Little Willie trench beside Hohenzollern Redoubt during the Battle of Loos on 2 October 1915. For a while it was thought that he had been taken prisoner but nothing more was heard of him.

London lawyer Godfrey Pope (born 1885) left for Ceylon in 'the rubber boom' of 1910 and worked for another Dorsetman, Mr Pitfield, on the Kahawattee and Serepama estates. In 1913 he bought a half share of the Arangalla Estate in Matala district. He had joined the Ceylon Planters' Rifle Corps and was refused leave to depart for the European war while a native uprising was a possibility.

Captain Albert Victor Pope (born 1887) joined the 14th (King's) Hussars in India and returned to England, to Bisley, as 'the best revolver shot in the Army' having scored 315 hits from 324 shots. In November 1915 he arrived in Basra with the India Expeditionary Force in Mesopotamia, making an impossible attempt at taking Baghdad from the Turks, which ended with a broken force falling back exhausted to Kut-el-Amara. It took more than a year to turn the tide and reach Baghdad, in March 1917; 'It is a city full of mosques and minarets, and looked a fine sight as we passed it with the sun setting behind the mosques.' They went on up the Euphrates, to take Ramadi, and Pope later led the advance-party of a force which continued across snow-covered mountains in Persia to the oil port of Baku on the Caspian Sea, in a secret raid against Turks and Bolsheviks in July 1918.

Jack Pope, Lieutenant John Allen Pope (born 1888), joined brother Godfrey in Ceylon. He returned with a colonial contingent and enlisted in the King's Royal Rifle Corps. Having fought at Ypres and in the Battle of Guillemont, on the Somme, he 'was invalided home, suffering from shell-shock and gastritis'.

Tenth son, Major Decimus Pope (born 1889), won the Military Cross while fighting in France with the Signal Service of 8th Army Corps. He was one of

Major Alfred Rolph Pope (1870–1951) of the Dorsetshire Regiment

Lt-Col Edward Alexander Pope (1875–1919) of the Welsh Regiment

Sergeant George Clement Pope (born 1876) of the 1st Volunteer Battalion, the Dorsetshire Regiment

Captain Charles Alfred Whiting Pope (1877–1917) of the Royal Army Medical Corps

Sub-Lieutenant William Eldridge Pope (1881–1901) of the Royal Navy

Second-Lieutenant Percy Paris Pope (1882–1915) of the Welsh Regiment

Private Godfrey Pope (born 1885) of the Ceylon Planters' Rifle Corps

Captain Albert Victor Pope (born 1887) of the 14th (King's) Hussars

Lieutenant John Allen Pope (born 1888) of the King's Royal Rifle Corps

Major Decimus Pope MC (born 1889) of the 8th (King's Royal Irish) Hussars

Captain Cyril Pope (born 1891) of the Bedfordshire Regiment

the survivors of a group of officers blown up by a shell on 9 January 1917 near Boulogne. A colonel and a major died of their wounds and Decie Pope lay in hospital with a wound in the right thigh. He had been thrown through the air. Providentially, 'another splinter had gone into my pocket, smashed my pipe, and, after going through my tobacco pouch, landed in the centre of a thick notebook.'

Captain Cyril Pope (born 1891) went with the 1st Battalion, the Bedfordshire Regiment from resistance to Home Rule in Ulster to the battles in Belgium as Field Marshal Sir John French's 'Contemptible Little Army' marched towards German invaders in August 1914. He was taken prisoner, in a wood in the dark, when he went up to a group of German infiltrators 'thinking them to be my own men'.

Back at home, sister Elizabeth Kate Pope (born 1879) worked in the bandage depot at Dorchester Military Hospital and managed the Stratton and Grimstone Coal and Clothing Clubs. Violet Mary Pope (born 1880) married Captain Alan Roderick Haig-Brown, the youngest son of the headmaster of Charterhouse School, who was killed at Achiet-le-Grand in northern France on 25 February 1918.

The family also had to recover from a post-war disaster much nearer home. On 18 November 1922 the Dorchester Brewery was gutted by a spectacular night fire, after which Rolph Pope – known as 'The Major' – rebuilt the buildings and the company. His eldest son, Cecil Pope, returned to Dorchester from Fuller's Brewery in Chiswick. By 1925 they were able to claim 'a Phoenix-like replacement, second to none, the most modern and hygienic in the country.'

With the death of Alfred Pope's brother, Edwin Pope (1845–1928), it was the size of the 'Millionaire brewer's will' that made national news. Popes remain at Wrackleford. Eldridge, Pope plc saw out the millennium with Jeremy Pope as managing director and Christopher Pope the chairman, from 1988.

Alfred Pope looking down on great-grandson Christopher Pope, at the Dorchester Brewery, with Lyme Regis author Ann Jellicoe in 1985

WRAXALL MANOR

Lawrence — Busk — Inchmore

In the Middle Ages the lands at Wraxall, a parish north-west of Maiden Newton, were owned by the Stawel and Bampfield families. The farm was leased by the Lawrence family.

William Lawrence (1579–1640) rebuilt Wraxall Manor in about 1620, with high mullioned windows and chimneys on the four gable-ends. He married Elizabeth Gibbes and their eldest son, William Lawrence (1611–81), became a lawyer. Having married Martha Sydenham, from Wynford Eagle, producing another William Lawrence, he then fell out with her.

Martha was described by Oxford gossip Anthony Wood as 'a red-haired buxom woman whom he esteemed dishonest to him'. The dispute led to Lawrence – already a minor poet – writing a work on Marriage, sub-titled 'by the Morall Law of God vindicated against all Ceremonial Laws of Popes and Bishops destructive to Filiation, Aliment, and Succession, and the Government of Familys and Kingdomes'. Two parts were published, in 1680, but the third failed to appear due to 'disturbances at the press'.

Wraxall Manor providing a Jacobean backdrop for the opening meet of the Cattistock Hunt in about 1948

Wraxall Manor in 1985

William Lawrence had also written on *The Heavenly Divorce; or, our Saviour divorced from the Church of Rome his Spouse.* He also pontificated on the royal succession, with a detailed argument supporting the Duke of Monmouth's claim to the throne, in the Right of Primogeniture, though he was safely dead long before the ill-fated Western Rebellion which attempted to bring this about.

In the twentieth century the Manor was the home of William Gould Busk, and Captain R.D. Busk, followed by Major P.E. Inchbald.

WYNFORD HOUSE

St Maur – Zouche – Sydenham – Best – Wynford

The presence of an eagle as the symbol of Wynford Eagle goes back to Norman times when the bird was the emblem of Gilbert de Aquila whose huge estates were managed from his invasion headquarters at Pevensey Castle, Sussex. The St Maur and Zouche families were followed by Thomas Sydenham in 1545. He came to the old manor house from Combe Sydenham, Stogumber in Somerset. Great-grandson William Sydenham rebuilt the house in 1630 and brought up a family of five tough and articulate sons. The eldest of the five, Colonel William Sydenham (1615–61), was Governor of Weymouth in the Civil War and a leading scourge of the county's Royalist rump. The other four brothers also fought for the Cromwellian cause.

They suffered a barbaric and traumatic outrage when their mother, Mary Sydenham, was murdered in her home by a Royalist, Major Williams, in July 1644. The killing was avenged the following year when Colonel Sydenham received the surrender of the King's Army in Dorset from Sir Lewis Dyve. Colonel Sydenham personally and summarily put Major Williams to death.

The other notable brother was the physician Thomas Sydenham (1624–89) who had enlisted in 1642 and was wounded and imprisoned in Exeter. He later made his name across Europe, as author of ground-breaking *Observationes Medicae*, in 1676. This incorporated his earlier *Methodus Curandi Febres* and included a detailed account of the gout with which he had suffered since 1649. His descriptions were also the first adequate attempts at providing a written diagnosis of complaints and conditions as diverse as chronic bronchitis, influenza, chorea, scarlet fever, measles and hysteria. For smallpox he advocated the cooling method of relief and for shivering fevers he pioneered the use of bark. Uniquely, he noted the periodic and varying intensity of recurrent diseases, which we would call epidemics.

Dr Thomas Sydenham (1624–89) of Wynford Eagle was thc world's first epidemiologist

The third William Sydenham lost the family seat in bizarre circumstances by offering it in a lottery in which tickets were restricted to selected friends and family. The plan went awry when the young female winner went off and married Doyly Michel of Kingston Russell House. They sold the house to another neighbour. Sydenham tried to renege on the arrangements and was imprisoned in Dorchester Gaol where he died in 1738.

The lasting name from this unlikely succession was the arrival of a High Court judge who, as Lord Wynford, took his name from the property in 1829. Samuel John Best, 7th Baron Wynford (1874–1943), and his son Robert Samuel Best moved the family seat to a new Wynford House, on the site of a Roman villa half a mile up the valley.

INDEX OF FAMILY NAMES AND HOMES

Abington - Compton House
Adye - Merley House
Aldred - Sydling Court
Alington - Crichel House
Aleyn - Purse Caundle Manor
Arundell - Chideock Manor
Ash - Merley House
Ashley - Saint Giles House
Ashley-Cooper - Saint Giles House

Baker - Ranston
Balfour - Branksea Castle
Bankes - Kingston Lacy House and Wolfeton House
Barnes - Purse Caundle Manor
Baskett - Dewlish House
Batten - Upcerne Manor House
Beaufort - Canford House
Beckford - Stepleton House
Bedford - Kingston Russell House
Beech - Hammoon Manor
Benson - Branksea Castle
Bentham - Forde Abbey
Berkeley Portman - Bryanston House
Best - Warmwell House and Wynford House
Bindon - Lulworth Castle and Waterston Manor
Bingham - Bingham's Melcombe
Blount - Canford House
Bond - Barnston House, Creech Grange, Post Green and
    Tyneham House
Bosworth Smith - Bingham's Melcombe
Boucher - Thornhill House
Bourke - Chettle House
Bower - Iwerne Minster House
Boyden - Dewlish House
Boyle - Stalbridge Park
Bragge - Childhay Manor and Sadborow
Brett - Mapperton House
Bridge - Bridehead
Bristol - Sherborne Castle
Broadrepp - Mapperton House and Melplash Court
Browne - Frampton Court
Brune - Athelhampton Hall
Bruning - Melbury House
Brymer - Ilsington House
Bubb - Eastbury House
Buckler - Melplash Court
Bullivant - Anderson Manor and Parnham House
Busk - Wraxall Manor
Butler - Woodsford Castle

Calcraft - Rempstone Hall
Carrell - Lytchett Matravers House

Carter - Kingston Russell House and Waterston Manor
Castleman - Chettle House
Cavendish-Bentinck - Branksea Castle
Cecil - Cranborne Manor and Lytchett Matravers House
Chad - Branksea Castle
Chafin - Chettle House and Waddon House
Chaffyn-Grove - Waddon House
Charles II, King - Trent Manor
Cheverell - Chantmarle
Cholmondeley - Anderson Manor
Christie - Branksea Castle
Churchill - Minterne Magna and Round Chimneys Farm
Chyke - Tyneham House
Clare - Loders Court
Clavell - Barnston House and Smedmore House
Clay-Ker-Seymer - Hanford House
Cochrane - Athelhampton Hall
Colville - Loders Court
Compton - Mapperton House
Conran - Bettiscombe Manor
Constantine - Merley House
Cooke - Athelhampton Hall
Cooper - Saint Giles House
Corbett - Waddon House
Cork - Stalbridge House
Courtenay - Canford House

Daccomb - Stepleton House
Damer - Came House and Milton Abbey
Daniell - Clifton Maybank
de Bruyn - Ranston
de Bryan - Woodsford Castle
de Childhay - Childhay Manor
de Crewkerne - Childhay Manor
de la Lynde - Winterborne Clenston
de Mauley - Canford House
de Melplash - Melplash Court
de Mohun - Hammoon Manor and Poyntington Manor
de Montmorency - Dewlish House
de Pentheny - O'Kelly
de Redvers - Loders Court
de Rothesay - Highcliffe Castle
de Stepleton - Stepleton House
Devine - Iwerne Minster House
Digby - Minterne House and Sherborne Castle
Dillon - Dewlish House
Dodington - Eastbury House
Dorchester - Milton Abbey
Doughty - Upton House
Douglass - Duntish Court
Drax - Charborough Park
Duff - Ilsington House

Eldon - Encombe House
Ellenborough - Warmwell House
Erle - Charborough Park
Estoke - Barnston House
Evans - Forde Abbey
Eyre - Sadborow

Farquharson - Eastbury Court
FitzGibbon - Waterston Manor
Fitzpaine - Woodsford Castle
Folier - Melbury House
Foster - Branksea Castle and Warmwell House
Fownes - Stepleton House
Foy - Duntish Court
Fox - Melbury House
Fox-Strangways - Melbury House
Frampton - Moreton House
Frampton-Hobbs - Moreton House
Freke - Melcombe Horsey
Frost - Childhay Manor
Fulford - Toller Fratrum

Garth - Ilsington House
Gascoyne-Cecil - Cranborne Manor
Gaunt - Gaunt's House
Gerard - Parnham House, Trent Manor and Waddon House
Glyn - Gaunt's House and Iwerne Minster House
Goodden - Compton House
Govis - Waterston Manor
Grant - Frampton Court
Gratrix - Anderson Manor
Greathed - Uddens House
Grey - Kingston Maurward House
Gribble - Kingston Russell House
Grogan - Bingham's Melcombe
Grosvenor - Motcombe House
Guest - Canford Manor
Guilford - Sydling Court
Gundry - Melplash Court
Gwyn - Forde Abbey

Hambro - Merley House and Milton Abbey
Hamely - Saint Giles House
Hamilton - Merley House
Hanham - Purse Caundle Manor
Hardy - Kingston Russell House
Hardye - Sydling Court
Harmsworth - Athelhampton Hall
Harris - Hurn Court and Uddens House
Hawy - Compton House
Hayward - Creech Grange
Herbert - Purse Caundle Manor
Herring - Herringston and Poxwell Manor
Heryng - Herringston
Herynge - Winterborne Clenston
Hody - Parnham House
Hohler - Trent Manor

Holford - Duntish Court
Holles - Loders Court
Hood - Loders Court
Hopwood - Bingham's Melcombe
Hornby - Chantmarle
Horsey - Clifton Maybank and Melcombe Horsey
Hoskyns - Purse Caundle Manor
Howard - Lulworth Castle, Poxwell Manor, Waterston Manor and Woolbridge Manor
Horsey - Clifton Maybank and Melcombe Horsey
Huntingdon - Ilsington House
Hussey - Edmondsham House
Hutchings - Sandford Orcas Manor

Ilchester - Melbury House and Woodsford Castle
Inchmore - Wraxall Manor
Isaac - Anderson Manor
Ismay - Iwerne Minster House

Jeffrey - South Lytchett House

Ker-Seymer - Hanford House
Knight - Hammoon Manor
Knoyle - Sandford Orcas Manor

Labouchere - Mapperton House
Lane - Bloxworth House and Poxwell Manor
Lang - Purse Caundle Manor
Langham - Bingham's Melcombe
Law - Warmwell House
Lawrence - Creech Grange, Tyneham House and Wraxall Manor
le Breton - Loders Court
le Poure - Sandford Orcas Manor
Lees - Post Green and South Lytchett House
Lindsay - Stepleton House
Littlehales Baker - Ranston
Livingstone-Learmonth - Hanford House
Llewellin - Upton House
Long - Athelhampton Hall
Long-Wellesley - Athelhampton Hall
Lundbeck - Kingston Russell House
Luttrell - Poyntington Manor

Makepeace - Parnham House
Marlborough - Round Chimneys Farm
Malet - Poyntington Manor
Malmayne - Saint Giles House
Malmesbury - Hurn Court
Maltravers - Lytchett Matravers House and Melbury House
Mansel - Smedmore House
Mansel-Pleydell - Whatcombe House
Marney - Waterston Manor
Marriott - Sydling Court
Marston - Rempstone Hall
Marten - Crichel House
Martin - Came House

Martyn - Athelhampton Hall
Medlycott - Sandford Orcas Manor
Mellor - Bridehead and Upcerne Manor House
Mews - Purse Caundle Manor
Michel - Dewlish House and Kingston Russell House
Miles - Forde Abbey
Millar - Sydling Court
Milton - Milton Abbey
Miskin - Sydling Court
Mohun - Wolfeton House
Monro - Edmondsham House
Montagu - Mapperton House
More - Melplash Court
Morgan - Mapperton House
Morton - Anderson Manor and Winterborne Clenston
Motley - Kingston Russell House
Mount Batten - Upcerne Manor House

Napier - Crichel House
Nepean - Loders Court
Newburgh - Waterston Manor
North - Sydling Court

Oglander - Chantmarle and Parnham House
Ormonde - Woodsford Castle
Oxford - Ilsington House

Parke - Thornhill House
Paulet - Melplash Court
Phelips - Clifton Maybank
Phillips - Athelhampton Hall
Pickard - Bloxworth House
Pickard-Cambridge - Bloxworth House
Pinney - Bettiscombe Manor and Racedown
Pitt - Encombe House, Kingston Maurward House, Melcombe Horsey, Rushmore House and Stepleton House
Pitt-Rivers - Melcombe Horsey, Rushmore House and Stepleton House
Plecy - Saint Giles House
Pleydell - Whatcombe House and Winterborne Clenston
Pleydell-Railston - Whatcombe House
Plunkett-Ernle-Erle-Drax - Charborough Park
Ponsonby - Canford House
Pope - Tyneham House and Wrackleford
Portarlington - Milton Abbey
Portman - Bryanston House
Pretor - Bettiscombe Manor
Prideaux - Forde Abbey

Raleigh - Sherborne Castle and Upcerne Manor House
Reymes - Waddon House
Rhodes-Moorhouse - Parnham House
Richards - Smedmore House and Warmwell House

Rivers - Rushmore House
Robinson - Parnham House and Stepleton House
Rodney - Merley House
Rogers - Bryanston House
Roper - Forde Abbey
Rose - Rempstone Hall
Ross-Skinner - Warmwell House
Russell - Kingston Russell House and Tyneham House
Ryder - Rempstone Hall
Ryves - Ranston

Sadler - Warmwell House
Salisbury - Canford House, Cranborne Manor
Sampford - Melbury House
Samways - Toller Fratrum
Sandwich - Mapperton House
Sauer - Parnham House
Savage - Bloxworth House
Savile - Chantmarle
Sawbridge Erle Drax - Charborough Park
Scott - Encombe House
Servington - Edmondsham House
Seymer - Hanford House
Seymour - Bryanston House, Trent Manor and Upton House
Shaftesbury - Saint Giles House
Sheridan - Frampton Court
Sidney - Sydling Court
Skinner - Dewlish House
Slade - Hammoon Manor
Smith - Sydling Court
Southborough - Bingham's Melcombe
Sprat - Parnham House
St Maur - Wynford House
Stafford - Woodsford Castle
Stalbridge - Motcombe House
Storke - Trent Manor
Stradling - Compton House
Strangways - Melbury House, Waterston Manor and Woodsford Castle
Strode - Parnham House
Stuart - Highcliffe Castle
Stuart-Wortley - Highcliffe Castle
Sturt - Branksea Castle, Crichel House
Suffolk - Lulworth Castle and Waterston Manor
Sydenham - Wynford House

Tabor - Anderson Manor
Temple - Eastbury House
Thimbleby - Wolfeton House
Thornhill - Thornhill House
Tiarks - Melplash Court
Tichborne - Upton House